IL142

(1999)

£3

The
Anthropology
of Real Life

The Anthropology of Real Life

Events in Human Experience

Philip Carl Salzman

McGill University

WAVELAND

PRESS, INC.

Prospect Heights, Illinois

For information about this book, write or call:
Waveland Press, Inc.
P.O. Box 400
Prospect Heights, Illinois 60070
(847) 634-0081

Cover Photo:

Ja'far Shirdel, Dadolzai lineage, Yarahmadzai tribe, Baluchistan (1968): loving and devoted family man; conscientious upholder of tribal values and lineage solidarity; judicious and respected leader; considerate and generous host; sweet-tempered and pleasant companion: a man anyone would be happy to know.

Contents

Acknowledgments

An anthropologist often works as a solitary researcher and scholar, going alone to the field, reading and writing on his or her own, and teaching her or his classes independently. But this seemingly individual anthropological activity is possible only because of the institutional support of colleges and universities, research funding agencies, and professional bodies, and because of the collective support of the community of past, present, and future anthropologists whose contributions make up past, current, and future knowledge, and who have provided and will provide the audience for the individual's contributions. I am thus indebted, and wish to thank Antioch College and the University of Chicago, where I was educated, and McGill University, where I have been employed. My research in Baluchistan has been funded by the National Science Foundation, the Canada Council, the Social Sciences and Humanities Research Council of Canada, and McGill University, and in Sardinia by the Social Sciences and Humanities Research Council of Canada, the Wenner-Gren Foundation, and McGill University. Behind these august institutional names have been many individual teachers, colleagues, peer reviewers, and administrators who have invested their valuable time, effort, and financial resources in supporting me and advancing my work. In Sardinia, my research was encouraged at the Istituto Superiore Regionale Etnografico in Nuoro, and was sponsored by the Istituto di Discipline Socio-Antropologiche of the Università degli Studi di Cagliari. I am grateful for all of this help which enabled me to carry out my research.

Anthropologists, especially in their role as ethnographers conducting field research, are also greatly indebted to those people who are the subjects of our field of study, and among whom we learn about events in human experience and about culture and social position. In pursuing our ethnographic research, we usually go and live among a population, commonly a population unfamiliar and foreign to us. We depend upon people's hospitality in receiving us, uninvited guests though we are. We rely upon their patience and tolerance in the face of our inevitable

ignorance and usually inadvertent rudeness. We count on their willing-
ness to teach us their ways, to share with us their precious understandings, even though their recompense for this effort is likely to be
nugatory or nil. Amazingly, almost always, the people upon whom we
descend do welcome us with hospitality, patience, and instruction. I
cannot say too much about the kindness and consideration offered to me
and my family by the Baluch and by the Sardinians. They opened their
lives to us and shared their selves and their knowledge, as well as their
resources and activities. I hope that some recognition arising from my
writings will repay, in small part, the debt that I owe my friends and
teachers in Baluchistan and Sardinia.

Few of us could have accomplished what we have, however modest,
without the support and encouragement of our families. My parents,
Norman and Leonora Salzman, provided me with every advantage within
their power. Joan David was my companion and support in Baluchistan.
Lisa Marlene Edelsward and I have collaborated in our Sardinian
research as in our lives. I dedicate this book to the future, to my children
Joshua Rawee and Leah Qiong.

Chapter One

Introduction
Events in Life and in Context

Ishvar Darji and Omprakash Darji, fictional protagonists portrayed by Rohinton Mistry in his acclaimed novel, *A Fine Balance*, are uncle and nephew whose fates were shaped by having been born members of the "untouchable" Chamaar leather-tanning and cobbler caste in a village near Bombay, India. Obliged by divine duty to pursue a "polluting" occupation, they were despised social outcasts, untouchables who were forced to keep their distance from members of "pure" castes. They began their lives in a huddling of rude huts beyond the margins of the clean caste village. Ishvar and Omprakash, like all untouchables, were refused entry to school and depended upon the often negligible hand-outs of upper caste farmers for their living. In their position at the bottom of the caste hierarchy, they were virtually powerless to influence their village society.

The quiet rebellion of Ishvar's father, Dukhi Mochi, against his caste fate led him to send Ishvar and his brother Narayan to a nearby town to learn tailoring, a "clean" profession, from a Muslim tailor. But

> their father's friends feared for the family. "Dukhi Mochi has gone mad," they lamented. "With wide-open eyes he is bringing destruction upon his household." And consternation was general throughout the village: someone had dared to break the timeless chain of caste, retribution was bound to be swift. (Mistry 1995:109)

As it turned out, retribution was not swift, but it was certain. While Ishvar remained in town, Narayan returned to the village and built up a good tailoring business, eventually replacing his hut with a "pukka" brick house. But "among the upper castes, there was still anger and resentment because of what a Chamaar had accomplished" (156). When Narayan demanded to cast his own vote during a national election,

1

rather than letting the high caste leaders vote for him, he was dragged off by upper caste "goondas," brutally tortured and murdered, and, that not being deemed sufficient, his parents, wife, and daughters were burned alive in their house. The only good fortune was that his son, Omprakash, was away in the small town learning tailoring with his uncle, Ishvar.

To avoid retribution in their natal village and to find work, Ishvar and Omprakash leave the small town, carrying little more than their tailoring skills, and go to Bombay. While in the big city they have escaped the iron grip of caste, but they still cannot control their own destinies. For they are caught up in the great events of 1970s India—Prime Minister Indira Gandhi's national "Emergency" and suspension of civil rights and liberties, the "beautification" program of destroying shanty towns, the carting off of people living on the street to work camps, and the forced vasectomies of the "family planning" population control program—that sweep them and many others like them along, contrary to their plans and contrary to their wills, and deform them and their destinies.

That people find themselves buffeted and even swept away by great and less-than-great events totally beyond their control is an old story. As the narrator of Saul Bellow's *More Die of Heartbreak* ([1987] 1997:110) puts it,

> . . . [E]very age has its gross hazards: The odds are heavy that when they pick up momentum you will be done in by them. Think of the Black Death or world wars or forced labor. When these get under way, few can hope to escape.

It is an old and well-known story, but also an important story to which we must attend, if we are to understand people's lives and fates. Even in my own, quite placid life, I have felt the reverberations of great events, and my life has been shaped by them. My grandfather on my mother's side, whose photograph in uniform I have on my desk, was a Master Sergeant in the Austro-Hungarian Army. Because he foresaw that the Great War (World War I) was going to be a bloodbath which would cripple an entire generation, he decided to emigrate to the United States. He dodged the bullet, but his wife did not, dying young in the Great Influenza Epidemic of 1919. She left young and frightened daughters, among them my mother, who has always carried the scars of this "abandonment" and loss. But if my grandfather had stayed in Europe and not emigrated, I might have been born a Polish or Austrian or Hungarian Jew. And would probably have been, as a three- or four-year-old boy, hauled off to an extermination camp and ended up a Holocaust statistic, rather than as a fortunate American and privileged professor in Canada. My mother and father reached adulthood and married in the Great Depression, struggled to provide themselves with the necessities of life, and always felt insecure about money, preferring in professional and family life to take the safest route—although they always managed to provide everything for me. I came of age in the aftermath of World War II, when the United States was the envy of the world, and, for North Americans, the world was their oyster. Riding just ahead of the post-war Baby Boom, welcomed to elite educational institutions, I enjoyed superb opportunities rarely available to those of modest talents. My good fortune was to be at the right place at the right time, benefiting from events that I did not author and could not control.

There are so many examples of the molding power of events. Where I live in Canada, but also in the United States, awareness has grown that the "discovery" of America and the spread of "civilization" was for the original inhabitants, the aboriginal peoples, in Canada now called First Nations, a disaster that transformed when it did not take their lives, misappropriated their lands, and seriously undermined their cultures. As for the Europeans who came to Canada, they often came not just to benefit from the great "discovery of America" and seek out better opportunities, but as a response to great and terrible events in their homelands, such as the Highland Clearances, in which Scottish crofters were forced off of their land so that it could be used for more lucrative sheep, the Great Potato Famine of Ireland, which made it impossible to survive on farms, the Massacre of Armenians in their conflict in Turkey, the Soviet repression of Prague Spring, Idi Amin's expulsion of East Indians from Kenya, the Islamic Revolution in Iran, the flight of the Boat People escaping the conquest of South Vietnam, and ethnic cleansing that sent Bosnians fleeing.

WHEN IS AN "EVENT"?

I would define an event as a sequence of actions and consequences. This is a broad and encompassing definition, purposely vague. This definition accommodates events large and small, momentous and insignificant. The "great events," for example the Irish Potato Famine or the Russian Revolution, are made up of literally millions of smaller events taking place at particular moments and places. While part of larger sequences, it is these smaller events that often have direct and immediate effect, such as an infection that leads to the death of one's mother.

Of great interest for us is the impact an event has on people's lives, the way it redirects lives, shapes them, terminates them, liberates them. The point is that people do not live in static, stable environments with constant, predictable conditions. In real life, things happen, and these things sometimes impose circumstances that transform people's lives.

Sometimes these events, although crushing, are known and understood, because in particular places droughts, floods, famines, depressions, and warfare return from time to time. Thus events express lives, manifesting the forces that underlie people's lives. Exploring events shows us what those lives are like.

Other events are unknown, or of a magnitude previously unknown. Sometimes all, and sometimes some people can adjust, adapt, and hang on, riding out the new circumstances, hoping for a return to the old conditions or at least to a new stability. Sometimes some people are broken—losing their jobs and property, losing their influence and standing, losing their minds or their lives—and never recovering. Yet others flee to different ways of living in the new circumstances by taking on new identities and new roles, or flee to foreign places where they try to rebuild their lives or build lives anew.

WHERE YOU ARE CAN AFFECT THE EFFECTS: THE IMPORTANCE OF "POSITION"

Ishvar and Omprakash, trying gently to better their lives, were torn and swept away by events totally beyond their control. Their occupational move out of their given position in the caste hierarchy led to retribution, visited on their family and later on them. Here was an event, or several events, horrific in content, meant by the perpetrators to stay, not to advance, change. These events were "social control" in action, the application of force by those in power to maintain the existing order and their privileged position (Wolf 1994). In Bombay, Ishvar's and Omprakash's position as impoverished albeit skilled workers without property, with a minimum of money, and with no social standing, made them especially vulnerable to state programs of nonvoluntary beautification, labor, and family planning. Ishvar and Omprakash might have fared differently had they not been at the bottom of society—poor, uneducated, unconnected, powerless. Where one fits in society, one's position and standing, is likely to influence exactly how one is caught up by events in course.

While we must always look to people's positions to understand how they are affected by events, there are many aspects of people's positions, and some or all of these may not be relevant. The Great Flu Epidemic was not a respecter of position; while some were more vulnerable because of position, both high and low, great and small were struck down. Nor did great wealth, education, professional success, culture, or even demonstrated patriotism help the Jews of Germany, for all criteria for position were submerged by the Nazis in the master distinctions of "race," which we think should be considered ethnicity. Most of the well-positioned German Jews with the means to escape were nonetheless caught up in the Holocaust because, much to their surprise and shock, they were denied entry to Switzerland, the United States, Canada (Abella and Troper 1982), and most other countries, and thus consigned to the gas chambers. Interestingly, in the years after World War II, the survivors of Nazi concentration camps, whose tragic position one might have expected to elicit sympathy, continued to be refused entry into Palestine, the United States, and Canada, while German officers and escaping Nazis were admitted with enthusiasm. So "position" may count, but not always in predictable ways.

REACTING TO EVENTS:
CULTURALLY CONDITIONED RESPONSES

Ishvar and Omprakash were not "free individuals" once they left their village, for they carried their village and caste-based culture with them. They had certain ways of looking at things, thinking about things, and judging things that they had learned as they grew up, and to an extent they interpreted their experience in these terms (Geertz 1973). For example, even after they had learned tailoring and moved to the city, they still identified with their community, the Chamaar leather workers' caste. And they, or at least Ishvar the uncle, felt, and felt with a passion, that a man was not complete until he was head of a family, and that as his nephew's guardian, it was his responsibility to see to it that his nephew was properly married. These conventional understandings, elements of Ishvar and Omprakash's culture, led the two men to arrange with a Chamaar family back in their home village a marriage between Omprakash and a daughter of the family.

The two men, who wished to follow well-established caste procedures for getting married, returned to their home region and its ongoing caste and power hierarchy. However, the members of the higher castes viewed them with anger, and this led to further misadventures and ultimately personal disaster.

This tragic consequence was brought about by a conjunction of (1) culturally conditioned ways of thinking and acting, (2) the constraints and opportunities provided by position in a hierarchy or as a member of one or another group or category, and (3) the pressures and possibilities of events as they sweep through time and across space.

It seems clear to me that the consequences of the actual historical events portrayed by Mistry, for people like Ishvar and Omprakash, left an indelible impression on the real collective memory of the Indian polity and, among other reactions, a visceral revulsion against population control programs. In 1985, some years after Mrs. Gandhi's "Emergency," I attended a joint meeting on population in Jodhpur, Rajasthan, of the Sociological Society and the Population Council. I was rather amazed to hear in the papers and debates a unanimous rejection of any attempt to control population growth. Taking a positive line, the professors and researchers argued that "people are our most valuable resource." I knew that the outrages of the Emergency lay behind this very possibly counterproductive, blanket response. After the "great event" of the Emergency, the Indian world was irreversibly changed.

Culture provides a foundation block in other "great events" as well. The Holocaust drew upon long-standing European anti-Semitism, itself based upon the characterization of the Jew as the anti-Christian, who, in rejecting Christ and thus God, aligns himself with the Devil (Goldhagen 1996:ch. 1). However, many German Jews were caught up in Holocaust, failing to escape when they might have, because they defined themselves as German, were devoted to German culture, and were loyal to Germany. These German Jews drew on certain elements of German culture, while the Nazis drew on others. We must not assume, then, that German culture or any other particular culture was or is a totally unitary, coherent, consistent vision. Every culture contains beliefs or values or ways of associating which do not fit comfortably with other equally well-established beliefs, values, and ways of associating. In eighteenth- and nineteenth-century India, for example, there existed together distinct and logically contradictory bases of governance: a political hierarchy of kings, maharajahs, and Kshatria warriors; a ritual hierarchy of Brahman priests, clean castes, and untouchables; and the hierarchy of otherworldliness led by propertyless ascetics (Burghart 1978). Political practice often involved negotiating the logical incompatibilities to arrive at a workable compromise among the parties in diverse positions of power and authority.

The multiple and potentially conflicting elements in any single culture are more than logical irregularities, for they reflect complex realities on which that culture is based. If we look at a "simple" tribal society such as the Nuer (Evans-Pritchard 1940) of the southern Sudan in the first and second decade of this century, we can see that the Nuer emphasized in their culture the principle of descent from a common male ancestor as a central defining feature of group formation and political solidarity. Yet the realities of Nuer life involved also (1) people sharing villages and territories, (2) commonalities or differences of position, work, and thus interests among people of different generations, (3) individual and family mobility across space, (4) marriage ties between families, and (5) amorphous religious congregations. So the Nuer not only had lineage groups based on descent, but also, cross-cut-

ting those lineage groups, community and territorial groupings of people living together, age groups in age set organization, the distinction in communities between lineage members and other residents, bilateral kinship ties reflecting connections between children and both their mother's and father's kin, and groups of worshippers following prophets.

A similar *multiplicity* of productive life is found behind the singular cattle idiom of ritual life and identity. The Nuer were obsessed with cattle; they were always thinking about cattle, talking about them, dreaming them, conducting rituals involving them, and literally identifying with them. But the reality of Nuerland was that cattle, while good to think, were not enough to eat. So the Nuer spent much of their time producing other food—such as millet that they grew in their villages, fish that they trapped and speared in the rivers, animals that they hunted, and vegetables that they gathered—not so good to think but quite good enough to eat. The Nuer liked to think of themselves as pastoralists raising cattle, but they were also cultivators, fishermen, hunters, and gatherers. They valued cattle, but they also depended upon a cultural technology which provided them with the mental and physical tools to produce these other kinds of food.

A culture, in its multiplicity, provides for many eventualities. A culture, after all, is a way of living, and it must take into account more than its own selective vision of what is good; it must also take into account the variable and varying conditions and circumstances in different parts of the environment, and at different times. Things happen, and people need to draw on their culture to cope with the things that happen. So, in addition to seeing a culture as a particular and partly arbitrary vision, we can also appreciate culture as a repertoire of multiple conceptual resources, a kind of mental tool kit, from which we can select those elements which best serve us in the face of current events (Salzman 1978b, 1981).

In trying to understand people who are living a different culture than ours, we cannot assume that what we see in a particular context or at a particular period is the totality of the culture. When we see a pitcher on the mound or a teacher at the lectern, we are not in a position to judge how or what they would do if they switched places, or as soldiers, or lovers, or ill patients. Similarly, what is manifest of a culture at a particular moment does not represent that culture's full repertoire, for many resources—productive technologies, values, ways of organizing, goals—will be recessive, in storage, waiting to be activated when they are needed. The Nuer, if they were to lose many of their cattle to raiding or rinderpest, could expand their millet cultivation, or if the fish catch were bad, could switch to hunting, although they might otherwise go years without hunting. And facing external political threats from Arab slave traders and imperialist forces of the Anglo-Egyptian condominium government, the

Nuer of all tribes reached beyond the limitations of lineage and tribe to rally behind their prophets, who stood for the Nuer people as a whole. So when events sweep down on people, when epidemics, droughts, invasions, floods, or depressions lay waste the land, people mine their cultures, drawing on those alternative ways of organizing themselves, of providing security, of making a living, and of defending their values that are most effective in the threatening circumstances that they face.

CYCLES, TRENDS, AND ACTS OF GOD

From our point of view, with which people experiencing and affected by events might or might not agree, events can be considered as parts of cycles, trends, or acts of God.

If events arrive in a regular and somewhat predictable fashion, they can be considered parts of cycles. There are climatic cycles in which more or less regular variations lead to repeated events, such as droughts, hurricanes, and floods. For example, in desert regions, rain comes very little or not at all one or two years out of every five. That this is known by the inhabitants does not make it any less an event. In capitalist economies, recessions and depressions alternate with periods of expansion and wealth; in stock markets, "bear" market declines alternate with "bull" market increases. Stock market "crashes," called "adjustments" by stock brokers, can destroy people's savings and careers, and suicides sometimes follow. Malthus ([1798] 1959) thought that there was a population cycle, with population expanding exponentially while productive resources expanded only arithmetically, so that a discrepancy grew between numbers of people and the goods needed to support them, until warfare over resources or disease feeding on the weak killed enough of the surplus population to bring population and resources into reasonable balance. While we now know that changes in the technology of production and reproduction and in the culture of fertility can ameliorate Malthus's stark dialectic, the threat of Malthus's discrepancy, especially in developing countries, continues to haunt us.

Some great events are part of trends which lead to cumulative change in some places. Both the "sexual revolution" and "women's liberation" of the 1960s were consequences of a series of trends in North American industrial society, including the decline in infant and child mortality and in fertility, the lengthening of the life span, the shift of work out of the home, allocation of children to formal schooling, urbanization, mechanization of household processing and reduction of household labor demand, and provision of commercial services for requirements previously provided in households. The demographic, technological, and practical necessity for most women to devote themselves to reproduction, child rearing, and household production had gradually disappeared, just as most men no longer engaged in labor- intensive primary production on farms and in forests. The old division of labor no longer existed, and women's liberation from their outdated and marginalized roles led to a redefinition of gender roles and a fuller integration of women into the new institutions of post-industrial society.

The arrival of motorized vehicles, a "great event" of modern times, is part of a more general and long-term trend of mechanization, the replacement of human and animal muscle power by mineral and vegetable energy used to run machines. Among desert nomads in Arabia and beyond, trucks and motorcycles have replaced camels as "ships of the desert" (Chatty 1986, 1996). Water is brought to pasturing flocks in tanker trucks, and, for long distance migration, sheep no longer make arduous journeys on hoof, but are transported by trucks. In the deserts of Baluchistan during the 1970s, I saw tribal nomads gradually switching to trucks and motorcycles for travel. It was not unusual to see, bouncing over the sand dunes, four beturbaned and bewhiskered Baluch astride their Russian motor cycle, with a goat tied on the back, or crowds of Baluchi families, setting off for the great, annual migration from highland pastures to lowland date palm groves, crowded into the open backs of the tough Mercedes Benz dump trucks needed to get through the mountains. The culture of the camel was being replaced with the culture of the car, the camelherder replaced by the mechanic. Animal husbandry for transportation was being replaced by capital investment and commercial purchase.

Other formative events are unexpected and unpredictable, the results of processes too complex or too random for people to grasp. These are thought of as "acts of God" or of "nature." Great epidemics, such as the Black Death of bubonic plague, the Great Influenza Epidemic after World War I, and the AIDS epidemic of the 1980s and 1990s are examples. Irregular but devastating earthquakes, volcanic eruptions, and tidal waves, often destroying entire communities and even cities, sometimes killing large numbers of people and ruining the habitations and livelihoods of even larger numbers, also appear to be "acts of God."

I offer these three characterizations of events—as manifestations of cycles, as steps in a trend, or as an act of God or nature—as ways of providing an analytic context for understanding events. But the designation of any particular event has to be considered suggestive rather than definitive, for whether an event is seen as part of a cycle, a trend, or nature, is at least to a degree relative to one's perspective. For example, last Sunday my house started shaking and continued for ten seconds or so. There had been an earthquake with a measurement of 4.3 on the Richter Scale, with the epicenter not too far from my house. This was fortunately a minor event with little consequence for myself and my family and others in the region. But as far as I was concerned it was an act of God, coming "out of the blue" and for no reason that I could understand. But a geologist of eastern Canada might see this earthquake as part of a trend of continental settling or building or part of an adjustment cycle of the shifting of the earth's crust. Similarly, to many unwilling participants in a war, such as the Bosnian conflict, the war might seem a calamity of human intention rather than an act of God. However, Malthus ([1798] 1959) might have seen it as part of a population cycle, and a political scientist might see it as part of a worldwide trend of ethnic nationalism and the breakup of multi-ethnic polities.

CONCLUSION: EVENTS AND REAL LIFE

First, events can have formative and even determining effects on people's lives, and so must be a focus of exploration as we try and understand people in our own societies or elsewhere.

Second, events do not usually arise from nothing—although sometimes acts of God seem as if they do. Usually events are shaped by the positions people are in and the culture that they carry. So events must be considered in conjunction with position and culture.

Third, people respond to events not just from their pan-human qualities and their idiosyncratic characteristics, but also in terms of their distinct cultures. Each culture incorporates certain alternative modes of organizing, assessing, and responding; and people are able to draw on those modes that are most effective in responding to the events in which they are caught up. Cultures tend to be highly attuned to events that come in cycles, less so to events that are part of new trends, and even less so to unexpected acts of God.

Fourth, events often take on a life of their own, as the sorcerer's apprentice discovered to his dismay. Could Guttenburg have had any idea that his printing would be a critical step toward the mass distribution of newspapers, books, and magazines and the spread of the ideal of universal education? Did anyone, even its Nazi authors, imagine at its initiation that the campaign to rid Germany of Jews would end in the mass death camps of the Holocaust? Could anyone have known, joyfully participating in the sexual revolution of the 1960s, that the result would be more children born to unmarried mothers than to married mothers and fathers (as is the case in Quebec in the 1990s), and that a substantial portion of unmarried mothers in North America would be teenagers and even preteens? Events sometimes take on a life of their own, and people's lives, their cultures, and the world are never again quite the same.

Chapter Two

Events in a Middle
Eastern Desert

Deserts are inhospitable places for most people, because deserts lack the water necessary for production and life. Before modern technology made places like Palm Springs, California, habitable, not many people lived in deserts. In the Sahara, in Arabia, and in other deserts around the world, some people lived in oases, those rare places in deserts where water made them unlike the surrounding desert, capable of quenching thirst and sustaining cultivation. Other people used the desert, for example, to mine salt. For actual desert dwellers, we can look to *pastoral nomads* in Africa and Asia, people who move their households around in the desert as they raise livestock to make a living (Galaty and Johnson 1990; Barfield 1993; Fabietti and Salzman 1996).

Living in portable or easily constructed shelters, such as tents or brush huts, and dressing in distinctive ways, from the blue veils of men among the Tuareg to the turbans of Arabia and beyond, pastoral nomads present a colorful image of the exotic cultures so beloved by anthropologists and tourists. These pastoralists' nomadic "lifestyle" and their dependence on the camel, the ship of the desert, seem to set them off as a unique kind of people, caught up in an original and archaic culture pattern. These images and sentiments are probably shared by most of us from industrial societies, which is entirely understandable given our own ways of life and the geographical and historical distance between our cultures and those of pastoral nomads. Perhaps we have a right to enjoy these images and feelings when we consider *exotic others.* The pleasurable contemplation of the great panorama of colorful human variation is after all one of the joys of travel and of anthropology.

Pastoral nomads pursuing their lives in desert environs are not, however, entertainers; they have not chosen or maintained their way of

11

life because it is colorful or exotic. For them, their way of life is not at all exotic, but natural and everyday. To them, their way of existing and being human is obvious and right, and our way of life would seem strange and exotic. Perhaps we, as observers of other cultures emphasize too much the differences between different peoples and their cultures, thus overly exoticizing what should be seen as normal ways of living similar in many respects to our own (Keesing 1994). In looking at pastoral nomads, maybe we could equally well begin not by stressing their differences from us, but with the opposite assumption, that they are much like us, that we share much as human beings, members of human society, and carriers of human culture.

Pastoral nomads, after all, face the same problems that most everybody else faces. Children are born helpless and have to be taught language and rules of living. People have to make a living and supply themselves and their families with the necessities of food, shelter, and clothing, and with the tools necessary to provide those things. Security against injury and death, and of property, have to be guaranteed as much as possible. Illness has to be countered and disability and death coped with. People have to establish ways to cooperate with each other in making a living and defending their lives and property, and people must find a way of relating to and responding to the forces of the universe.

Pastoral nomads are trying to solve these problems and cope with the difficulties of doing so, as are all of us. Thus, I would suggest that we try to look at pastoral nomadism as real life, rather than as culture in its folkloric aspect, as colorful and exotic customs. *Culture*, including the specific cultures of particular groups of pastoral nomads, can be seen as a set of shared, symbolic tools for attacking the problems of real life (Salzman 1981). In this sense, each culture provides guidelines and examples (Geertz 1973; Ortner 1973) for getting along together, bringing up children, making a living, defending life and property, and relating to the spiritual world.

A further complication, I would argue, is that a culture cannot provide guidelines for only one set of activities, one form of organizing, one way of making a living. As we shall see, because of the alternation of drought and flood, war and peace, scarcity and plenty, and isolation and contact, the circumstances of life for any population is likely to change and change again over time. So each culture must provide a range of possible responses, alternative models of action, for coping with the various conditions that repeatedly prevail and with which the people must deal (Salzman 1978b, 1981). Along with the ongoing demands of everyday life, these challenges and changes manifest themselves in flurries of activity that we can, for convenience, call events. By examining these events, we can gain insight into the life of pastoral nomads, into their guiding culture, and into that multiplicity in their culture which facilitates flexible and effective response to real life.

We cannot, however, look at real life among pastoral nomads in general, because pastoral nomads—like members of all general categories, such as hunters, cultivators, and fishermen, men and women, Africans and Asians—differ from one another in major ways. Some pastoral nomads live in harsh deserts, while others live in mountains or lush plains; some consume what they produce, while others trade in markets; and some are members of tribes, enjoying considerable political autonomy, while others are peasants, largely under the control of state agencies. So we must pursue our investigation by exploring the nature of a particular group of pastoral nomads. I want to present the case I know from my own field research, the pastoral nomads of northwest Baluchistan.

THE DESERT OF BALUCHISTAN

Baluchistan means "land of the Baluch," and is a vast contiguous area divided by national boundaries into southeastern Iran, western Pakistan, and southwestern Afghanistan. The majority population speaks the Baluchi language, a western Iranian language closely related to Kurdish, and influenced by Persian in the west and Urdu in the east. The harsh desert of which Baluchistan consists is only sparsely populated, the population divided among small agricultural oases, herding camps in the desertic plains and mountains, and small trading and administrative centers.

I chose a particular group of Baluchi pastoral nomads to study, the Yarahmadzai (Yar-ahmad-zai = descendants of Yarahmad) of the highland Sarhad in the north of Iranian Baluchistan (Salzman, Forthcoming B). When anthropologists do *field research*, they usually focus upon one particular people, and their portrait of that people is called an *ethnography*. Ethnographic field research is commonly based upon a general strategy called *participant observation*, in which the researcher lives among the population studied for a considerable period, preferably a year or more, and to a modest degree is able to participate in and experience the life of the people. By being present, the anthropologist is able to observe directly events unfolding which both influence people's lives and reflect the nature of local life. *Direct observation* by the anthropologist provides him or her with firsthand information about people's actions and expressions as they anticipate, contribute to, experience, and react to the event taking place. By observing an event, whether usual or unusual, planned or unplanned, large or small, harmful or beneficial, or of uniform or differential effect amongst the population, the anthropologist can see people's strategies for coping with situations, their patterns of association, cooperation, and conflict, and the goals they are pursuing and the values they are exhibiting. Of course, anthropologists complement direct observation with conversations, discussions, and interviews, in which people express, although at second-hand, their views, feelings, and reactions, in short, their perspectives on the event and what it means to them. One of the main strengths of participant observation is that it allows the anthropologist to cross-check many different kinds of information, such as the degree of correspondence between what people say to each other and what they say to the anthropologist, what people say on different occasions, what people say and what people do, and what people do on different occasions. The anthropologist also has the opportunity to observe and record the diversity of views, values, and strategies among the population, for no population is uniform and no culture is monolithic.

My field research among the Yarahmadzai tribe consisted of twenty-seven months of residence, in three stints, during the period 1968-1976. I used as a residential and social base, and a primary object of study, the herding camp of Ja'far, and, as did the other members of the camp, I lived in a tent and migrated from place to place as the camp was relocated. While I spent much of my time in the camp, watching events as they unfolded, following people in their activities, and discussing with people what they were doing and why, I also lived briefly in the camp of the tribal chief, visited many other herding camps of the tribe, and travelled to the date groves for the summer residence. In addition, I had a residence in Khash, the small administrative center on the western edge of the tribal territory, to which I retreated one or two days a week for trips to the bathhouse, post office, and stores where I bought supplies. There, as well as in Zahedan, the provincial capital, I met government officials. I was also able to visit and investigate other populations, such as the nearby Kords (Kurds) of the Kuhi Taftan mountain range in the north, and the oasis peoples of the Saravan region to the south. In all of these investigations, my direct observation of various events—such as migration, negotiating a contractual group, the splitting (fission) of a herding group, drought, deaths, feuds, and state campaigns of control—proved particularly instructive.

MIGRATION

Yarahmadzai camping groups, consisting of a few to several dozen households and their black goathair tents, could be seen repeatedly through the year breaking camp, taking down and folding their heavy tents and packing up other belongings, loading them onto reluctant and protesting camels, and then migrating off toward the horizon. But we must not let our imaginations run too far. Yarahmadzai nomadism did not involve romantic penetrations into unknown foreign lands. Rather, migration was almost always limited to the home territory held by the Yarahmadzai tribe. So the various locales of residence were almost always known well by some members of any camping group. Furthermore, these migrations were not manifestations of "wanderlust" or expressions of exuberant liberty, but were deliberate practical strategies to achieve a number of goals, usually related to economic production.

Commonly the main goal was to insure the welfare of the livestock, the flocks of goats and sheep (with goats predominating by two to one) and the camels. Relocation of the camp was usually intended to move the livestock closer to good pasturage, to good water, and away from any flocks thought to be diseased. *Migration* was thus an adaptation to a desert environment where edible grasses and bushes, and water, were sparsely and erratically distributed over the landscape. Mobility allowed the tent-dwellers to move to where, at that moment, resources such as pasturage and water were available. Other purposes of migration included moving away from dirty sites, moving away from the vicinity of sick animals, moving to the location of cultivation, and avoiding conflict by moving away from crowded areas or enemies. Between October and June, many Yarahmadzai herding camps would migrate between a half-dozen and a dozen times; some migrations would be quite short, under a mile, while others would be twenty, thirty, or even more miles.

In addition, there were migrations between different environmental areas. Yarahmadzai herding camps, which remained on the Sarhad Plateau during most of the year, would migrate down off of the plateau to reside during July, August, and September at their date groves in the easterly, lowland drainage basin, the Hamuni Mashkil. For this migration, at 120 miles the longest of the year, the flocks were left behind on the cooler plateau in the care of shepherds, and only the camels, as burden animals, accompanied the tribesmen and tribeswomen for the date season.

Migration was an event repeatedly generated by Yarahmadzai themselves in the pursuit of their own purposes. Because migration was aimed at spatial displacement to increase benefit and reduce risk, it can be considered a purposeful, *adaptational* event. For the Yarahmadzai, migration was always a significant event. Its purpose was integral to making a living and providing security. But it was always an arduous undertaking, depending on much human muscle-power. The greatest work and effort of migration was prior to the actual move itself. When and where to migrate were questions that involved ongoing and complex information collection and negotiation. People leaving the camp acted as scouts, surveying conditions in the countryside. And visitors to the camp were politely grilled for information. Herding camp members were constantly discussing environmental conditions and migratory options. Decision making was democratic, with advocates of different views attempting to rally public opinion in the camp, and the camp headman, *master*, responsible for eliciting a crystallization of public opinion and providing final enunciation of it. It was common for weeks of debate to precede a migration.

Difficulties in coming to a collective decision about when and where to migrate resulted not only from imperfect knowledge about environmental conditions; difficulties also inevitably arose from the differences of interests and priorities of different camp members. First, different individuals had different profiles of livestock: some had more goats, some had more sheep, and some had more camels. As each species required different kinds of pasture and different amounts of water—grazing sheep required grass and browsing goats and camels needed different kinds of bushes, and the small stock needed more water, more frequently than the camels—different locations were inevitably better for one species than another. Thus, different locations were differentially attractive to owners with different herd profiles. Second, individuals varied in their dependence on livestock: some had all of their wealth tied up in livestock and no other sources of income, while others had fewer livestock and equal or greater amounts of income from cultivation, trading, or migrant labor. Those people with commitments to cultivation, whether as owners or laborers, had a geographical anchor in their fields which constrained their enthusiasm for far flung migration. Irrigated fields had to be watered at least every ten days. And those people with few animals were not inclined to heroic migrations on their behalf. Third, individuals had close kin in other locales, and different individuals were attracted to different locales for this reason. Fourth, those people working off-and-on as migrant laborers or traders preferred to stay close to the lines of transportation, so that they could leave for work and return to camp relatively easily. In sum, each individual in the camp had a different set of interests and preferences from each of the others. Thus each had different needs in regard to timing and destination of migration. Coming to a decision about migration involved constant negotiation and an arduously forged compromise among the camp members.

For purposes of public consultation, men were deemed the representatives of households and household herds. Although there was general circulation of people of all ages and sexes through the camp, especially among close relatives, men tended to congregate and work with men and women with women. Men were constantly discussing and negotiating practical matters, such as migration. And so were women. Some women owned livestock of their own, and all women had a stake in the livestock managed by the active, senior male of the household on behalf of the household. In addition to the women's views about managing the livestock, views frankly shared with male household members and sometimes males outside the household, there were issues and circumstances relevant to migration on which women acted directly and decisively.

Observing the actual events, we can see women's influence clearly. One factor always of importance in the life of the camp was access to water for household use: drinking, cooking, washing eating implements, washing the person, and washing clothes. As collecting the water from wells, streams, or rain-fed pools was a task allocated to women, they were the authoritative judges of the water situation: whether the water sources were close enough or too far, whether the water was sweet enough, and how long the water would last. When the women were arguing that the water source was too far away, the water too dirty or salty, or soon to run out, this was a strong reason in favor of migration to a locale with better access to sweet water. I have seen this pressure lead to early migration.

Another factor was labor. If many men were away from the camp and the labor of migration would fall too heavily on the women, they would, barring extreme circumstances, oppose migration until a larger complement of men was present. A third factor was the availability of men for decision making. Customarily, the headman of the camp enunciated public opinion and specified the compromise plan of action. But in his absence, others had to take the initiative. On one occasion, the wife of the headman, responding to the loss of stock through illness, initiated a migration, which was carried out in spite of the shortage of labor. A fourth factor was the attachment of women to kin living in other camps. Women sometimes pressed for migration which would bring them closer to the camps of their kin. If women went on extended stays with kin in other camps, their husbands would sometimes advocate, using camouflaging rationales, migration closer to those camps.

In the Sarhadi desert, nobody could know ahead of time whether or where rain would fall and vegetation would grow. The rainfall was very erratic; some years there was less than one inch, while others saw ten times as much; some years or some months rain fell exclusively in the south of the tribal territory, some years or months in the north, or in the west, or east. So the uncertainty in decision making about migration resulting from the diversity of purposes and need for compromise was exacerbated by uncertainty in the environmental setting, due especially to the sparsity and irregularity of precipitation and consequent unpredictability of availability and location of pasture and water. As a consequence, for environmental reasons, camp migrations were spatially irregular and unpredictable, one going north, and the next south, and the next, who knew? Migrations on the Sarhad Plateau were a catch-as-catch-can, week-by-week adaptation to micro-environmental variations. The exceptional, predictable migration was the annual one between the plateau and the stable, permanent date groves.

So many elements of Baluchi nomadic society and culture were manifested in migration that it was a paradigmatic event for Yarahmadzai and other Baluchi nomads, an event that stood for and represented, both practically and symbolically, their way of life. Particularly attuned to migration and the nomadic life, both reflecting it and making it possible, was Yarahmadzai *material culture*, the equipment needed for nomadic practice, and especially the knowledge and skills required for making the equipment. For example, weaving by Yarahmadzai women produced goathair tents for use as shelter; rugs both plain and fancy of various sizes for sitting, sleeping, and praying; decorated luggage bags of many kinds for carrying tools, supplies, and materials during migration; elaborate camel saddle blankets and leads; and simple storage bags of many types, for foodstuffs such as grain and dates and other supplies. Tribal women wove these from the wool and hair of their own animals. These woven goods were usually used by household members or campmates of the weavers; they were not directed to any market. When not in use these rugs and bags were folded flat and stacked neatly in one pile at the end of the tent.

Even Baluchi clothes were well adapted to tent living. The long, loose shirt hanging to men's knees and women's ankles, and the voluminous long pants of both sexes, gathered with a draw string at the waist, as well as the women's large, loose veil hanging from the head to the ankles (but not covering the face unless the sides were purposely pulled together across the face) provided both protection from the elements in all seasons and modesty in the midst of crowded, camp living. Leaving the camp for a more private place, usually behind a sand dune, to perform excretory functions, or to wash or shave, a Baluchi man or woman had only to squat down to be surrounded and cut off from view by their loose clothes. Baluchi clothing operated as a small, portable tent, loose enough to be moved out of the way for whatever the activity was, but so voluminous as to cover the person from the shoulders to the ground and block any view. (Not that anyone was looking; the Baluch were too delicate and polite to do so. If someone inadvertently came near you, they "did not see" you.) Baluchi clothes were so loose once the draw string was slackened, that people had no trouble changing all of their clothes without ever showing an inch of skin. They would simply insert their fresh clothes inside of the ones they were wearing, slipping on the new clothes, and then taking off the outer layer of old clothes! With the proper Baluchi clothes, life could go on and modesty maintained even in a crowded tent. Young Baluchi men who returned from migrant labor in the Persian/Arabian Gulf wearing jeans found that they were very unsuitable for tent life. Just sitting on a rug for a while with one's knees up made one long to get rid of tight and binding jeans and don loose, Baluchi trousers.

RENEGOTIATING THE SOCIAL CONTRACT

As we have seen, Yarahmadzai tribesmen and tribewomen lived in herding camps of anywhere from a few up to forty households and tents. The camp was the residence group, the face-to-face community of neighbors. However, the members of these camps were not present by virtue of long-established relationships, nor by any cultural rule that specified who would belong. Rather, these camps were established and renewed each year by purposeful agreement, by annual contract; each year a new agreement would most likely see some members from the previous year leave and new members arrive. The herding camp was thus a consciously constructed group. Every year the reconstituting of the camp, of its residence group, was an important event. In this case, where the event was regularly generated by the social arrangements of the group itself, we can call it a cyclical, structural event.

The contract that established camps was not *the* social contract of the Yarahmadzai, but one of the elements in the larger "constitution" upon which tribal society was based. The contract focused on a narrow but important economic consideration, the establishment of a collective flock and the hiring of a shepherd. Thus those people representing households were acting as livestock owners, and the shepherd was their employee. Each camp was expected to have one and only one flock. The community of livestock owners and the households they represented were thus, technically speaking, an epi-phenomenon of the herding contract. If your sheep and goats were in the contractual flock, you were in the camp community and could reside with other community members; if your livestock were not in the contractual flock, you were not in the camp community and could not reside there.

At the end of every spring, the contract was renegotiated. It was a little like Christmas; everyone was thinking about who had been good in the previous year and who had been bad. Had the shepherd been good, moving the flock around for good pasturage, insuring the health of the animals and their offspring, and cooperating with the livestock owners? Had this or that livestock owner been bad, causing trouble for the shepherd, not cooperating with the other owners on migration policy, and not carrying his share of the work? Who should be included in the next year's contract and who should be excluded? There were environmental considerations as well. Did the next year look like a good one or a drought one? In a good year the flock could be large, because there would be enough vegetation within reach to support it; but in a drought year the flock had to be small, for the pasturage within walking vicinity of the camp would be severely limited. A small flock meant fewer household flocks could be included, and thus there would be fewer households in the camp. It also meant less compensation for the shepherd, who received the bulk of his pay per animal. So an adult, professional shepherd might not even want to take the job in a drought year, not unless the terms of the contract were made attractive. Clearly, the renegotiation of the herding contract, including as it did the welfare of the animals and the membership of the camp community, was a serious and worrisome occasion for all concerned.

While formally the camp community was constituted by the herding contract, the underlying reality was more complex. The truth is that there were first-class and second-class community members. Those camp members who were connected by a number of formal relationships other than the herding contract formed a core of allies, and those others who had no close ties were socially and politically somewhat peripheral. Perhaps the most important ties were common lineage membership, that is, descent from a common ancestor through the male line, or *patrilineal descent*. Those individuals, both males and females, sharing descent from a relatively recent common ancestor, such as a great grandfather or great, great grandfather, shared a normative and practiced commonality and solidarity. Among the Yarahmadzai, relations of descent were vested with responsibility for welfare and defense; people closely related had to support and provide aid to one another and also had to stand together and if necessary fight together against more distantly related people.

Often overlapping and reinforcing lineage ties were *affinal ties*, relationships through marriage. The Baluch, as most Middle Eastern peoples, had a well-established preference for marrying close kin; they said, "Marry a cousin and you know what you are getting." In marriage you were getting not only a spouse, but also a father-in-law, mother-in-law, brothers-in-law, sisters-in-law, and so on. If you married a cousin on your father's side, a patrilateral cousin, it was certain that your in-laws would be your close lineage mates, as well as your uncle and aunt and cousins; even if you married a cousin on your mother's side, a matrilateral cousin, you would be marrying lineage mates if she married one of her close lineage mates. The result was that some camp members had relationships built up of many overlapping ties, or multiplex relationships, and had also shared residence and cooperated in many labor activities over the years. These camp members had built up commitments and obligations to one another over time and had confidence in one another, knowing that help given at one time would be paid off later on. Those camp members who were close lineage mates and affinal kin, and who shared a history and most likely a future, formed the core of the camp. The camping group in which I lived most of the time had an ongoing core of members from the Dadolzai (= descendants of Dadol) lineage. Other people, from other lineages, with marriage ties to non-Dadolzai families, through herding contract joined the camp from time to time, but left after shorter stays than members of the core group, and were less likely to rejoin than members of the core group (Salzman 1992:81, Figure 3).

Being a member of a herding camp easily can be a temporary thing. Nomadism makes possible not only moving from place to place, but also moving from one social group to another, from one residence group to another. No one is stuck in one group just because he or she happens to be there, or her or his house or land happen to be there. Mobility of the household allows a shifting between social groups. People who do not get along can leave, or be sent away, relatively easily. Thus tensions which arise through conflict can be dissipated through separation; people do not have to live with people they feel are enemies, their angers constantly poisoning their lives and the community life. The ingenious custom of the Yarahmadzai herding contract enhanced this group shifting by specifying a short, one-year term of commitment, and provided no end of narrow technical reasons for the breaking of residential ties: "Oh, we would love to have you with us next year [yeah, right], but [we will say that] our camp flock will have to be much smaller and your household flock is too large to include." Or, "We would love to remain part of your camp next year [sure we would], but [our excuse is that] your shepherd is not suitable for my flock." So people could leave camps without the breaking of social ties and with a minimum of hard feelings. In this way, the Yarahmadzai make the most of the social benefits of nomadic flexibility, while at the same time optimising the ecological and productive efficiency of the herding camp by reshaping the camp according to the needs and resources of each particular year.

FISSION

Both migration and contracting among the Yarahmadzai were intentional events, generated purposely, if arduously, by these Baluchi nomads drawing on their culture. But life was not always so manageable, and events were not always desired and expected. The desert was not exclusively a showcase for people's intentions and plans. For example, the break-up of groups, whether herding camps or lineages, was often unexpected, undesired, and regretted. This fissioning of a camping group or lineage disrupted people's lives, for they depended upon these groups for production, security, and welfare. The break-up of a group in the Sarhadi desert was equivalent to, in North America, the closing of a factory or the loss of a town's municipal status.

I want to describe briefly one particular event that I observed directly, the fissioning of a herding camp. This happened in spring 1973 in the camp in which I was living, the camp led by Ja'far and dominated by members of the Dadolzai lineage. The dramatic break-up of the camp happened physically at the moment when the camp members, leading their camels, loaded with all of the tents and baggage, began to set off on a migration. As one set of people and camels headed off in a southerly direction, fully expecting everyone else to follow, the others split off and headed toward the east. I could not believe my eyes; this long established camping group, well esteemed by other tribesmen and tribeswomen, "my" camping group, in which I had lived five years before, was breaking up, fissioning, unexpectedly, as I watched.

In order to understand why people had done what they had done, leading to the fission, I talked to many of the parties involved. Conveniently for me, key figures in the decision making happened to be close friends and informants of mine. I learned that there were two critical elements that led to the break. One was a disagreement about migration policy. Members of one faction had good sized herds on which they depended heavily for income. They always wanted to pursue pasture in an aggressive fashion, migrating whenever the opportunity for improved pasture arose. The members of the other faction had fewer livestock and depended also on cultivation, migrant labor, and trading for income. These people wanted to insure that their livestock were well cared for, but did not want to engage in heroic efforts, frequent and arduous migration to distant destinations, for what they saw as small or doubtful marginal gains. Both factions felt that the other faction was not accommodating enough.

The second element that contributed to the break was the effective absence of leadership to sound out public opinion in all factions and bring about a satisfactory compromise for all camp members. The esteemed camp leader, Ja'far, had for at least a month prior to the migration been very ill, in great pain, with stomach ulcers. He had not been able to do his job, and thus each faction in the camp was left to evolve its own vision, position, and plans. When the split came, no one was more surprised than Ja'far.

It was obvious to me from the first moment that the split had divided factions not based only upon migration policy. The factions also were divided on lineage affiliation. The Dadolzai had four sub-lineages, each descended from four sons of Dadol. The factions were based upon these sub-lineages, the "aggressive migration" faction being made up of members of the Shir Delzai, the descendants of Shir Del, son of Dadol. The other faction consisted of members of the Dust Mahmudzai and their close matrilateral kin and affines among the Shadi Hanzai, both also sons of Dadol. So in addition to disagreements about migration policy, there was also closeness of kin ties holding members of each faction together and apart from the other. Because close kin ties carry the obligation of political support, members of each faction felt that they had to support their sub-lineage mates in opposition to members of other sub-lineages. Ja'far, in my first discussions with him, said that he felt that he had to stick with the Shir Delzai, because they were his lineage mates. So sub-lineage solidarities and oppositions exacerbated the disagreement about migration and contributed to the split.

After a couple of months, during which Ja'far continued to be unwell, the two factions continued separately. But because Ja'far was ill, and could not migrate far, the camps ended up not far from each other. There was a lot of regret about the split, for the Dadolzai prided themselves on their solidarity and tranquility, and when Ja'far regained his health somewhat, there were initiatives to bring the two factions back together. At this point, Ja'far, using a standard manipulation of descent idiom, denied that he had ever acted out of solidarity with one sub-lineage, arguing that all camp members were Dadolzai and that there was no difference amongst them. After some recrimination against one of the supporters of the aggressive migration policy, and apologies from that individual, who from then on, that year at least, kept a low profile in the camp, the factions reunited and became a single camp and community once again. But the dramatic split of the camp reminded members that unity was very fragile and an inadequate dedication to solidarity and compromise could easily lead to an unanticipated and unwanted fission.

DROUGHT

Every few years there is a drought in the Sarhadi desert. Little or no rain falls, and, as a consequence, there is little plant growth, and thus little for the animals to eat. Animals that have not eaten cannot lactate and cannot provide milk for their young offspring or for human consumption. Without milk, lambs and kids die, and human beings go hungry and sometimes sicken and occasionally die.

Climate is by its nature variable, not only from season to season due to celestial positioning, but also from year to year. Temperature, wind, and humidity vary, but above all, in the arid regions where water is scarce, precipitation varies. While the average, annual rainfall in the Sarhad was 5.1 inches (1963–67, 1971–76), the amount of rainfall in any given year could range from less than 2 inches to more than 10 inches.

During the drought of 1965 and 1966, there were 1.5 inches of rain the first year and 2.1 inches the second. Then in 1971 there were only 1.6 inches of rain, and 1973 was only a bit better with 2.8 inches. These droughts presented severe challenges to the Yarahmadzai. During drought years, large numbers of the lambs and kids died; for example, in 1971, 55 of the 92 recently dropped kids and lambs in the flock died. The consequences carried over into the following years, when there were few young, lactating females, and the overall supply of milk was down.

Milk was a staple of the Yarahmadzai diet. It was the main source of protein and fat, calcium and other nutrients, in the largely meatless meals of these Baluchi nomads. Most pastoral nomads do not eat much meat. Their flock is their capital, a kind of renewable resource, on which they depend for milk, wool and hair, and offspring. So the object is to conserve the flock, not to kill animals and eat up the capital resource. It is true that among most pastoralists—those raising animals for wool are the exceptions—flocks consist largely of bearing-age females, with most male animals sold for meat, burden, or traction, or ritually sacrificed and eaten for occasional religious holidays. But everyday cuisine in the Sarhad of Baluchistan did not include meat; Yarahmadzai nomads would eat meat perhaps once a month. So milk was a critical foodstuff for them.

Milk was drunk fresh and soured, alone or in tea or with flatbread, which was the other main staple. This bread was made from one of several different whole grains and baked in one of four different thicknesses, using one of four different techniques, at least once a day by Yarahmadzai women. A typical, main meal among the Yarahmadzai consisted of a bowl of liquid—commonly milk, half fresh and half sour, perhaps with some Indian spices or hot peppers mixed in, with a little ghee (clarified butter) floating on top—into which the substantial bread was broken to soak up the liquid. The milk-soaked bread was eaten with one's fingers. This dish, called *hatuk*, which to a Westerner might sound unappetizing, was in fact very palatable, as well as being sustaining and nourishing. In the absence of fresh supplies of milk, Yarahmadzai were often able to turn to their stores of dried milk solids, which were either prepared and stored by themselves, or purchased elsewhere in the tribe or in the bazaar of the regional, administrative town. In extremity, bread could be soaked in water spiced with hot peppers.

It is obvious from the centrality of bread in Yarahmadzai consumption that these nomads, as with many others throughout the Middle East, relied upon sources of production other than their livestock. In fact, Yarahmadzai had always been involved in various kinds of production. They cultivated a bit of grain and a lot of dates and also hunted and gathered. Until 1935, these Yarahmadzai were also famous raiders, riding outside of Baluchistan to steal livestock, valuables, and even people from Persian villages and caravans. This predation brought a good supplementary income to the tribe. Since accepting the suzerainty of the Iranian state in 1935 and the suppression of raiding, they switched to migrant labor and mobile trading/smuggling. And in recent decades irrigation cultivation has expanded; this added a more reliable source of crops to the unreliable rainfall cultivation based on the construction of small mud barriers at the bottom of run-off channels. Thus the Yarahmadzai had always engaged in various kinds of production, never relying on one only. Their economy was generalized, or mixed, rather than specialized; it was a multi-resource economy.

One of the advantages of a multi-resource economy was that it provided a certain amount of security. If one kind of production failed, people were able to turn to the other kinds and be sustained by them. For example, a drought would undercut pastoral and rainfall cultivation production and income, but irrigation and date palm cultivation drew on ground water, and thus were little affected by annual variations in precipitation. Production of grain and dates thus continued to provide foodstuffs even in a drought. So did migrant labor and trading excursions, as did predatory raiding in the past. Furthermore, the tribesmen diverted attention and energy from the drought-struck pastoralism and rainfall cultivation to the production activities not affected by the drought, thus increasing income from the other spheres. In the early part of the century, this led to more raiding expeditions; in the second half of the century, to more trading and migrant labor expeditions. The date harvest during the drought year of 1971 was particularly large, almost 50 percent higher than 1972, although how much was due to more intensive productive activity and how much to natural conditions is difficult to say. But what is clear is that the high level of date production made up, to a degree, for the losses in the pastoral sector from the drought.

In sum, a diversified or multi-resource economy provided security because people were not dependent on one kind of production alone. If one kind of production broke down, the others continued to provide necessities. The multi-resource economy was particularly useful because the process was dynamic. People could with minimal difficulty shift their efforts from one sphere to another as was necessary or opportune, emphasizing one sector at one time and another at another, according to the prevailing circumstances. By so doing, the multi-resource economy allowed people to optimise their situation. Drought did not destroy the Yarahmadzai, because they could shift to other productive activities and survive on their income. Similarly, when the government cracked down on raiding or trading, the Yarahmadzai could rely on their livestock, cultivation, and migrant labor. The multiplicity of production gave the Yarahmadzai the flexibility to deal with events that reduced or shut down one or another of their productive activities.

TWO DEATHS

In 1967–68, Shams Hartun was a member of the herding camp led by Ja'far. I knew her family well. Her brother Shams Adin was my closest friend and helper in Baluchistan. Her mother Zar Bonu loaned us her tent when we returned in 1972–73. Shams Hartun was a Dadolzai and one of the core members of the camp. She had multiple and ongoing ties with many members of the camp. She had married her father's brother's son, Malik Mahmud; when he fell ill and died, she married his brother, Rahim Dad, but he too died. Her marriages had brought her children, but also misfortune in the loss of two husbands.

Shams Hartun's first marriage, to her father's brother's son, was, from a structural point of view, ideal. Baluchi preference in marriage was close kin, on the father's side if possible. The reason for marrying close kin is that you know the spouse and the family, and you have other important ties with them. By marrying this way, the bride and groom are associated affinally, by marriage, with close kin by descent, and thus are building on an already well-established solidarity. The reason for marrying on the father's side is so that the bride and groom both belong to the same lineage, and the children will thus belong to the same lineage as their matrikin as well as their patrikin.

Shams Hartun and Malik Mahmud did not choose each other as spouses; even less did they date and fall in love. Rather, their parents arranged the marriage between them. Those being married must give their consent as part of the formal Islamic marriage ceremony, but they usually have agreed ahead of time to go along with their parents' wishes. Shams Hartun was undoubtedly quite young when she married; Baluchi girls traditionally married between twelve and sixteen years old, commonly before puberty. (This practice tended to preclude any problem of illicit, pre-marital sexual relations.) When I asked young women if girls should not pick their own spouses, they said, after considerable giggling, "How would we know who would be a good husband? Our fathers know." In choosing brides, it is the mothers who usually predominate in their selection.

Marriage was not just a personal relationship; rather, it was a partnership in at least two senses. First, marriage was an alliance for the establishment of a new household. Each household was an economic enterprise, a unit of production as well as of consumption and sexual reproduction. In order to support itself, it had to be effective in production. So the partners would ideally have been hard working, skilled, devoted, smart, and well connected to other people. In other words, marriage was an extremely practical matter rather than a primarily sentimental one. Second, marriage was an alliance between two families. A person's in-laws, his or her father-, mother-, brothers-, and sisters-in-law became close relatives. If they were a good family, they could be an invaluable resource. If they were not a good family, they could be an infinite source of trouble and difficulty. So choosing well at the beginning was crucial in many practical ways. When one married, in a sense one married an entire family. This was also the logic behind Shams Hartun's marriage to her dead husband's brother, not an uncommon practice in this part of the world. Among other things, marriage to the brother of a deceased husband insured that the children, who belonged first and foremost in their patrilineal descent system to the family of her husband, were raised by a man who was closely connected with the children and would look after their interests.

Shams Hartun was fortunate to have been nicely fertile. She gave birth to six children from her first two husbands. Children were high priorities among the Yarahmadzai, as is true in most agrarian societies. There were many practical reasons for this. First, miscarriages, still-births, and infant and child mortality tended to be quite high, due to poor nutrition, poor sanitation, and the absence of modern medicine. So it was necessary to have a lot of pregnancies and a lot of children in order to insure a reasonable number of surviving offspring. Second, non-industrial agrarian economies were highly labor intensive; in the absence of powered machines, people depended primarily upon human muscle power to get things done. Every little task needed to be done by hand, from collecting and delivering firewood and water to grinding grain into flour. All manufacturing was done by hand. Transportation was often by foot, although animals were sometimes used. In short, there was a great deal of hard work to be done. The labor of children was required to get all of the tasks done. The more children, the more labor, the more production, the more there was for consumption. In short, children were needed for their labor contribution. Third, grown children provided political support for their parents. In tribal societies, each able man was a warrior, and numbers of men, both sons and sons-in-law, were political and military strength. Fourth, in societies without old age pensions and retirement homes, adult children provided homes for and supported aged parents. Having children was constructing one's own safety net and guaranteeing security in the future.

Shams Hartun was, I repeat, fortunate in her children. The Yarahmadzai love their children very much. They are very indulgent toward young children and kind toward older children. The love and concern devoted to children was not a facade constructed because they needed children and used their labor and depended upon them, but a genuine sentiment arising from parents' and other relatives' investment in children. Children were one of the main creative successes that people could have in this society. The status of both men and women rested on having children. A man showed his manhood by having children, and a women fulfilled her womanhood by having children. Full adulthood came only when one had children. Infertile couples were deemed both sad and ridiculous.

As a young widow, Shams Hartun faced a terrible dilemma. On her own, she could not support her household. Her parents and brothers helped her, but this was not a substitute for a husband who would be producing primarily for her household. When Shams Hartun married a third time, her husband was not of her immediate lineage group, and lived far away, in the provincial capital. She did not want to carry her children away from their home and kin or to subject them to a new step-father who might resent and mistreat them. Nor, I suspect, did she wish to burden her new marriage with such a potentially stressful influence as her four youngest children.

Fortunately, the collective nature of kin ties and the practical contributions of children provided Shams Hartun with a solution to her problem, a solution which we might call "fostering." She was able to place her young children in the households of close kin, all of whom lived together in the same herding camp, where they were able to make valuable labor contributions in return for being cared for and supported. Alluk, at fifteen years, lived with his uncle Mahmud Karim and worked as a shepherd; Tutonuk, at ten years, and Azimuk, at six years, lived with their married brother Abdul; and Zaruk, at eight years, lived with her grandmother Zar Bonu. This fostering arrangement was not unusual. Dust Mahmud, brother of Shams Hartun's deceased husbands, sent his daughter Marium, at twelve years, to live with Mahmud Karim and help in the household, and his son Mahmuduk, at ten years, to live with Shams Adin and work as camelherd. When for one reason or another parents could not care for their children, close kin were always ready to take them in. After all, they were close kin; they were, as they said, "one."

FEUD

On 23 August 1972, a greedy camel ate dates from a palm tree not belonging to its owner. This small event rapidly grew into a major feud rending the Yarahmadzai tribe asunder. The aggravated owner of the date palm took possession of the camel and demanded compensation for the dates eaten from the owner of the camel as a prerequisite for releasing the camel, which incensed the camel owner. The two men exchanged unpleasantries, and then blows. The owner of the camel got the worst of it. These two men were acting not only as individual agents on their own behalfs, but, due to being members in the Yarahmadzai tribal system, they were, whether intentionally or not, also acting as representatives of political groups based upon lineages. Each Yarahmadzai individual was a member of his father's, grandfather's, great-grandfather's lineage, and so on to the all inclusive lineage membership of the founder of the tribe, Yar Ahmad. Members of these lineages had collective responsibility for each individual member. An act of a lineage member to an outsider was deemed an act of all lineage members; an injury to a lineage member was deemed an injury to all members. Lineage members were obliged to defend one another, and to unify to fight outsiders. All lineage members had to contribute to compensation paid to an outsider for a wrong done by a lineage member. Vengeance could be taken against any lineage member for an injury or death caused by another member of the lineage. In this *segmentary lineage system* (Sahlins 1961; Salzman 1978a), individuals were not left on their own to fend for themselves, but were given security and protection by their lineage mates. The basic ethic was "all for one, and one for all."

The tribal security system worked by establishing that no individual or small group was "free game," attackable without response. Through collective responsibility, retaliation was certain. This gave pause to potential predators. And it was not only potential opponents that put the damper on thoughtless aggression or purposeful predation, but also allies. Lineage mates of potential aggressors knew that they would be dragged in and put at risk if one or more of their lineage mates acted imprudently. In order to avoid this, lineage mates acted to inhibit unruly, hot-headed, and aggressive individuals in their lineages. The ultimate sanction of a lineage against a member was excommunication, disenfranchisement. For example, a member of the Dadolzai who had murdered a random outsider, encountered in the deserts of Mashkel, in order to show how strong he was, was given no additional chances by his lineage mates. This time, they said, they would pitch in with compensation, but if he did it again, he was on his own; the Dadolzai would kick him out and not come to his aid. He did not do it again.

The camel owner and date palm owner mentioned above were members of different maximal sections of the tribe; the former was a Rahmatzai, the latter a Soherabzai. So conceptually two of the three major divisions of the tribe were in conflict. It did not take long for retaliation to take place. A group of angry Rahmatzai happened across several elderly and one young male Soherabzai and their female relatives. The Rahmatzai took the occasion to rough them up. The older men were highly respected elders of the Soberabzai and other Soherabzai were shocked at such disrespectful treatment. This incident led to parties of Soherabzai searching out Rahmatzai who had date groves nearby, although these individuals escaped before being caught. Soherabzai then ruined some wells in Rahmatzai areas. Word went out that groups were mobilizing for a major confrontation. I nervously accompanied a group of a hundred or more Soherabzai, armed with brass knuckles, sticks, knives, and hatchets, on their way to an isolated plain to confront an army of Rahmatzai. I was both disappointed and relieved when the opposing army did not show up.

By this time the *sardar*, chief, of the Yarahmadzai, Han Mahmud, had been alerted and had come to Mashkil to settle the matter. He met with the elders of the Rahmatzai and suggested a modest compensation for the mistreatment of the Soherabzai elders. The Rahmatzai leadership was intransigent, rejecting not only the payment of any compensation whatever, but also the leadership of Sardar Han Mahmud, who himself was Soherabzai, and even common tribal membership, saying that the Rahmatzai was a separate tribe. Needless to say, this attitude did not go far to settle the feud.

In fact, the feud between the Rahmatzai and Soherabzai continued for four years. Members of the Rahmatzai married to and living with Soherabzai moved back to their Rahmatzai lineage mates. Gangs of Rahmatzai and Soherabzai hatched plots to capture members of the other lineage and punish them. Various individuals were confronted by members of the other lineage and threatened, chased, attacked, and abused. Repeated attempts, including one in the government courthouse at Khash, the regional administrative center, by the Sardar and others to bring the parties together for settling the feud ended in outright brawls. The Sardar in 1976 finally collaborated with the government authorities in threatening anyone, from any lineage, who did anything, with jail sentences. This seemed to settle the matter at least temporarily. Not much later the fall of the Shah and the subsequent vacuum of power, to be discussed below, would draw the tribesmen and tribeswomen's attention.

As we have seen, the Yarahmadzai tribe housed two, somewhat incompatible kinds of organization. The lineages were collective, egalitarian, and decentralized, and they operated in terms of balanced opposition between lineages of the same size. At the same time, the chiefship of the tribe was individual, hierarchical, and centralized. There was structural inconsistency between the lineage system and the chiefship, and often a practical conflict between them. The chief stood for the whole tribe, while the lineages stood for their members against other lineages. In conflict, the lineages opposed one another according to genealogical opposition; but in settlement, especially when led by the chief, all lineages, those close and distant, allies and enemies, all contributed compensation to the victims, thus underlining the unity of all Yarahmadzai. The co-existence of the lineage system and chiefship provided Yarahmadzai tribesmen and tribeswomen with the option of emphasizing opposition, equality, and decentralization, when this suited their needs, and unity, hierarchy, and centralization, when this suited their needs. It thus gave them flexibility in their organizational stance, a capacity to shift to one or another formation as circumstances required.

ENCAPSULATION

In 1928, Reza Shah, the first Pahlavi king of Iran, sent an army into Baluchistan to "pacify" the unruly tribes and bring them securely under the control of the crown. Previously, during the latter part of the Qajar dynasty, the second half of the nineteenth and early part of the twentieth centuries, the Persian crown had been weak, and its political hold over distant provinces tenuous. The tribal regions of Iran, in the mountains and deserts which surround the central plateau and its Persian cities and peasant villages, had been beyond the effective control of the Persian state, the tribes functioning as independent political entities, fighting and making peace among themselves as they chose, treating with foreign powers, engaging in predatory extraction, both extortion and raiding, from peasant villages and commercial traders, and not paying taxes to the crown or sending recruits to the royal armies. Reza Shah set about changing all of that.

Reza Shah, beginning in the 1920s, conducted over the course of a decade successful campaigns against the Qashqa'i and Arabs in the southwest, the Lurs in the west, the Kurds in the northwest, and the Turkmen in the northeast, not only defeating these nomadic tribes militarily and bringing them under the control of the state, but forcibly sedentarizing them in villages with permanent housing that he made them build themselves. Reza Shah then turned his attention to the most remote region claimed to be part of Iran, Baluchistan. An army was sent in 1928 and succeeded, with the help of artillery and primitive bombing from early aircraft, in pacifying all of Baluchistan, except for the Sarhad. Led by the Yarahmadzai, who had earlier fought the British (Dyer 1921), the Sarhadi tribes resisted successfully, until finally settling and accepting the suzerainty of the Persian crown in 1935 (Arfa 1964). The settlement was dignified, but the reality was that the Yarahmadzai and other Sarhadi tribes had accepted defeat and lost their independence.

The Yarahmadzai were defeated but not forcibly settled. Their aged Sardar Jiand Han, the leader of the Sarhadi resistance, was exiled to the distant Persian city of Mashad. But a new Sardar, Hubyar Han, was allowed to take his place, and was provided a government salary. The Yarahmadzai lost their tribal name, becoming the Shah Navazi, "Shah Strokers," to symbolize the suzerainty of the Iranian king. This is the name they were using when I carried out my research. There were a number of important and substantial changes in the lives of the Yarahmadzai. Most obviously, they were not their own political masters, as they had been in the past. While they maintained their political structure of lineage system and chiefship, they were *encapsulated* (Bailey 1969, ch. 8) by a larger and more powerful political system which exercised a significant degree of effective control over them.

Raiding, which had usually been carried out against Persian targets, mainly peasant villages and trade caravans, was suppressed. This meant that there was no more income from raiding, which had been particularly important during times of drought and other economic shortfalls in the Sarhad. Without captured slaves to do agricultural labor, the tribesmen had to undertake this work themselves. It was the loss of income from raiding that led to a gradual increase in migrant labor and mobile trading and smuggling on the part of Yarahmadzai tribesmen. No longer able to dominate others through predatory raiding, the Yarahmadzai were forced to accept a subordinate position and sell their labor to bring in additional income. Trading and smuggling came later, as Yarahmadzai became more familiar with the nontribal world around them and more proficient in its ways. For most Yarahmadzai, these activities were not a new way of life, but a new way of earning supplementary income which allowed them to maintain their tribal life in the desert.

The political structure of the tribe also shifted somewhat. The chief, who in the past depended entirely upon his tribesmen and tribeswomen for support, now had new external resources. As the *middleman* between the tribe and the state, the chief took on new roles as an *intermediary*, acting as a channel for communicating messages between the state and the tribe, as a *mediator*, bringing the tribe and state to mutually acceptable compromises on courses of action, and as a *broker*, advocating to the state on behalf of the tribe and its needs. The chief was the recipient, on behalf of the tribe, of state largesse in the form of famine relief, agricultural equipment such as irrigation pumps, and infrastructural projects such as new roads. The chief enjoyed the status of the distributor of these valuable new resources. As well, the chief could expedite and facilitate various favorable decisions by the state and its bureaucracy for individuals or groups of Yarahmadzai, such as getting people out of jail and trading goods out of customs. This too brought the chief support by the tribesmen and tribeswomen.

The middleman position of the chief also had its risks. If the government was unhappy with the Yarahmadzai and their activities, it held the chief responsible. For example, the Gendarmerie, the Iranian National Police, initiated, while I was in the field, a campaign to disarm the tribesmen. This was a basic tactic of the state, which always claims the monopoly of coercive force. The Yarahmadzai chief was told that if he did not get his tribesmen to turn over their illegal guns, that is, ones without government permits, he would be held responsible and thrown into jail until they did turn them over. The chief then suffered the indignity of being driven around the desert, from one herding camp to another, in a Gendarmerie truck, with a detachment of soldiers, and having virtually to beg his tribesmen and tribeswomen to turn over hidden armaments. In this case, enough ancient rifles were unburied and turned over to gain the chief's release. But there were many cases, from other tribes in Iran, of uncooperative chiefs being removed from their positions by state authorities, and many cases of tribal chiefs being captured and sent into exile or executed (Barth [1961] 1986; Beck 1991; Beck, forthcoming).

Another change resulting from encapsulation was the shift in consciousness and identity. The Yarahmadzai and the Baluch in general became more religious, more assiduous in carrying out religious obligations, and tended to emphasize their religious identity as Muslims. They started sending substantial numbers of their children to religious schools, and some became mullas, learned religious leaders. They prayed more regularly, kept the fast, and increasingly went on the *haj*, pilgrimage, to Mecca. After his pilgrimage, the chief was addressed as Haji and referred to as Haji Han Mahmud, this religious title taking precedence over his secular title of Sardar.

There were two interrelated reasons for this increased emphasis on religion. One was the difficulty in sustaining old identities after encapsulation. Yarahmadzai could no longer emphasize being daring raiders and fearless warriors. And their pride in wrenching a living out of the harsh desert was undercut by the comparison of their poverty to the wealth of the Persians. The second was the inadvertent fact that the Yarahmadzai and the Baluch in general were Sunni Muslims, while the Persians were Shia Muslims (this split in Islam being a little like that between Catholics and Protestants in Christianity). Thus religion could be used as a defensive boundary between the conquered Baluch and the conquering Persians. Furthermore, while the Baluch could be shown to be politically and economically weaker than the Persians, they could claim, to their own satisfaction at least, that their religion was the correct one and that the Persians were in error. Some Baluch even went so far as to say that the Shia Persians were not really Muslims.

After the encapsulation by Reza Shah, there were two breaks in direct state control, corresponding to two changes in government leadership. In the first case, Reza Shah was dethroned and sent into exile by the Allies during World War II for being too friendly to the Axis powers. The tribes, which had seen most of their flocks die since their forced settlement, all breathed a sigh a relief, and left behind the sites of their settlements as they returned to nomadism again (Barth [1961] 1986; Irons 1975). Iran was divided into British and Russian spheres of influence,

with Baluchistan, on the border of British India, falling under its pur-
view. After World War II, with Reza Shah's son, Mohammad Reza Shah
Pahlavi on the throne, came a long period, under U.S. influence, of
rebuilding state control in the tribal areas, in some cases by military
campaigns. The Pahlavi regime lasted until 1978, when the Islamic revolution swept it away. In the vacuum of power during the aftermath of
the revolution, the tribes once again took political control of themselves
and their regions.

When the new Islamic government was establishing itself, conflict
broke out in Baluchistan. Persian Shias from Sistan in the northern
part of the province marched on the provincial capital to take control in
the name of the revolutionary government. This resulted in an armed
confrontation, in Zahedan, the provincial capital, between the Persian
Shia Sistanis and the Sunni Baluch. In this initial battle, the Baluch
successfully blocked the Sistanis from taking control. The tribes mobilized militarily to defend Baluchistan and establish their own control.
Meanwhile, the national government reestablished the national military and set about pacifying, once again, the tribal areas. The Islamic
government initiated and carried out successful military campaigns
against the Qashqa'i in the southwest, the Kurds in the northwest, the
Turkmen in the northeast, and they took control of Baluchistan as well.
In the aftermath of the conflict in Baluchistan, various tribal leaders
fled. The chiefly family of the Yarahmadzai went into exile in Quetta in
Pakistani Baluchistan. During this exile, the brother of the chief, Nezar
Mahmud, a friend and informant of mine, was assassinated. A few years
ago the government allowed the chief and the remainder of his family to
return to the Sarhad.

Encapsulation and decapsulation were events quite common in
this part of the world and elsewhere. For most of history, the agrarian
state was really just a concentration of military, economic, and symbolic
power that would extend its control territorially as far as it was capable,
usually claiming some kind of legitimacy for doing so. Its business was
really just to extract resources for its own consumption from the populations it controlled. One might characterize state officials and agents
as predatory thugs; certainly many of the local people who fell under
their control saw them that way (Gellner 1988). When the state was
strong, its control expanded geographically, encapsulating local populations; when it was weak, its control shrunk geographically, decapsulat-
ing local populations, leaving them free of state influence.

There were often regions, especially those poor and unproductive,
and difficult and expensive to control, such as mountains and deserts,
which for long periods lay far enough outside the reach of state centers
of power to remain independent. Baluchistan, a rugged and poor region,
halfway between centers of power in Iran and India, was one of these.

There, as elsewhere outside of state control, local populations would form regional political structures, which we call tribes, to protect themselves and also to expand at the expense of others.

When an agrarian state expanded and encapsulated a tribe, it usually allowed the structure of the tribe to remain, and governed through it, a convienient and cost-effective "indirect rule" like that favored by the British in its now defunct empire. Thus an encapsulated tribe, although no longer fully politically independent, retained the political structure to allow it to operate independently if the opportunity arose. But if the state were strong enough, it would often remove tribal leadership and replace it with its own representative and the structures of tribal decision making by state structures (Barth [1961] 1986; Bates 1973; Beck 1991), which went beyond encapsulation to what I would call *incorporation*, an integration of local structures with state structures. At this point, tribes have totally lost their political independence, and are tribes only in memory and perhaps in wish. Remaining after incorporation is primarily *ethnicity*, the identity of common background and a sharing of culture. Former tribesmen and tribeswomen, even if still nomadic pastoralists, have, in effect, become peasants, agrarian producers subject to state control (Salzman 1996a).

The next step of state domination may be cultural integration, the *assimilation* of tribesmen and tribeswomen into national culture, usually dominated and defined by the majority population. With cultural assimilation, the tribe increasingly becomes only a pale memory of the past. Alternatively, regional populations might use ethnic identity to mobilize politically as an ethnic block, in opposition to a state controlled by a different ethnic group. There is today some sign of this in Baluchistan. But the development of pan-ethnic consciousness also requires a suppression of tribal loyalties, and ethnic block political mobilization requires supra-tribal structures. The Yarahmadzai tribe faces a challenge, and the direction of its evolution is uncertain, even to the Yarahmadzai themselves.

MULTIPLICITY: A CONCLUDING REFLECTION

In dealing with events, people draw on their culture and act from their particular positions in society. But, as we have seen with the Yarahmadzai, culture is not limited to a single, unitary, obligatory way of doing things. Rather, culture usually includes a variety of ways of making a living, of organizing households, groups, and security, and of relating to the outside world. It is this multiplicity that provides people the flexibility to deal with and survive in the real world. The multiplic-

ity of society and culture offers alternatives—of production, organization, identity—from which people can select those most appropriate for
the conditions and circumstances that they face.

Cyclical variations in circumstances through time, variations of
peace and war, famine and plenty, and isolation and intermixing, may
see people shifting back and forth over time between segmentary division and chiefly unification, between external raiding or trading and
local pastoralism and cultivation, between tribal identity and ethnic or
religious identity, to mention some of the alterative patterns available
to and used by the Yarahmadzai Baluch. Cumulative changes over time
may lead to permanent shifts in a culture, with people drawing on the
elements of the culture most suitable and opportune in relation to the
new developments. For example, the politically encapsulated Yarahmadzai drew on their intrepid external excursions for extracting wealth
and their nomadism in their innovative shift to migrant labor and
mobile trading and smuggling. Focusing on events thus allows us to see
the complexity of cultures, the ways in which cultures are used, and the
way in which cultures evolve.

Chapter Three

Events on a
Mediterranean Island

To consider further the impact of events on people's lives, and the ways in which people's lives shape events, I want to take you to a large island in the center of the western Mediterranean Sea, the island of Sardinia. I want to tell you about life on Sardinia—where I conducted ethnographic field research from 1987–1995, living there twenty-eight months in total—because, reflecting on what I had seen, I was really struck by changes from year to year in the tenor of life, in what people thought and worried and talked about, in what led people to mobilize and to organize and to act as one event succeeded another, and in the mental and public landscape. But before I tell you about the flow of events and their consequences, I want to alert you to some of the basic patterns of life found in Sardinia.

LIFE AND TIMES ON A MEDITERRANEAN ISLAND

Far from being a people unknown to Europeans and discovered only recently by anthropologists, Sardinians have been caught up in major flows of Mediterranean history for at least three thousand years. Located about half way between the southern coast of Europe and the western coast of North Africa, Sardinians (who currently number around 1.5 million) have enjoyed the energetic attentions of Phoenicians, Carthaginians, Romans, Vandals, Byzantines, Saracen pirates, Pisans, Genovese, Spanish, Piedmontese, and finally Italians, who have traded, invaded, and occupied, except for brief moments between invaders of local independence and internal strife. Although lying 130 miles

west of continental Italy, Sardinia has been incorporated into the Italian
state for over a hundred years. The distinct Sardinian language is
derived from and close to Latin, but is mutually unintelligible with Italian; however, most Sardinians now also know standard Italian.

Through most of history up to the present, the great majority of
Sardinians lived in relatively isolated rural, inward-looking, nucleated
communities, "agrotowns," commonly with hundreds but many with a
thousand or a few thousand inhabitants. Aside from inhabitants of the
several small cities which developed over the last several hundred
years, Sardinians have lived either in lowland plains, the preferred
objects of invaders who established agricultural estates there, or in the
mountains, where Sardinians withdrew to escape the not-so-tender
mercies of occupiers. As is common for settlements in the European
Mediterranean, most Sardinian agrotowns are inland, many up on
mountain sides, avoiding the coastal malaria and sea-borne raiders and
invaders. Fearing the coasts and the sea, most Sardinians were farmers
or shepherds or both; the usual productive regime included wheat agriculture, sheep and goat pastoralism, and garden crops of beans (and
potatoes, after the discovery of the New World), vegetables, herbs, fruits,
grape vines, and olive and almond orchards. Production supported a
Sardinian variant of the Mediterranean food complex: flat bread and
pasta, beans, sheep's and goat's milk cheese, tomatoes, olive oil, and
wine, with the occasional supplement of air dried ham (prosciutto), mut-
ton, and almond sweets.

The Sardinian region of Ogliastra consists of the central portion of
the island's eastern mountains and lowland coastal plains. Most Ogliastrans have lived in towns up on the sides of mountains. As I based my
research in an Ogliastran town called Villagrande Strisaili (in Sardinian: Biddamanna Strisaili), and my students carried out research in
neighboring mountain towns, my description will focus on Ogliastran
highlanders in particular and Sardinian mountaineers in general, such
as the neighboring Barbaracini (from Barbagia, "the land of the barbar-
ians," as it was called by the Romans).

As elsewhere in the Mediterranean, the basic territorial and social
unit has long been the *comune* (plural: comuni; in Spain, the *pueblo*), or
municipality, which consists of a bounded territory at least partly suitable for agricultural production, within which is situated one nucleated
settlement and sometimes smaller settlements, *frazioni*, or rarely scattered homesteads or farmsteads. To get the idea of the form it might
help to think of a small city-state. In Sardinia, highland comuni had
large territories and were distant from one another. Each comune or
municipality was considered something of a world to itself. Each had
distinctive dress, bread, cuisine, and often dialect. Each comune formed
a closed social group: access to communal land was limited to members

of the community; marriage was endogamous, spouses being chosen primarily from within the community; and there were expectations of social peace, solidarity, and mutual aid among community members but not between members of different communities. Local identity and patriotism (in Italian: *campanilismo*, a reference to the local church bell tower, *campanile*) was very strong, and most Sardinians placed a high value on "belonging," on being a member of their comune.

With poor roads and great distances separating them, Ogliastran communities were isolated; the region of Ogliastra, itself poorly connected with the rest of the island, was called *un'isola nell'isola*, an island within the island. But isolation was only relative, for Sardinians were undeniably integral parts of European civilization: Ogliastrini, as the inhabitants are called, spoke a language based on Latin; they were Roman Catholics with the full panoply of local Church institutions, churches, priests, and nuns being present in every community; they had over the centuries been part of and operated to a degree under the laws of Roman, Vandal, Genovese, Pisan, Spanish, Piedmontese, and Italian states and empires. Differences between communities in "traditional" dress were in the nineteenth and twentieth centuries small variations in basic Spanish costume. Differences in cuisine between communities were variations on the general Sardinian version of the basic Mediterranean diet. Ogliastrini and other Sardinian mountaineers may have been distinct, but their distinct pattern was woven within the broader fabric of Euro-Mediterranean civilization.

DAILY LIFE IN THE MOUNTAIN
AGROTOWNS OF OGLIASTRA

Sardinian highlanders lived from day to day engaged in making a living, supporting their families, and managing extra-familial relations. These concerns were ongoing, whatever the impact of events (such as those described later in this chapter) as they succeeded one another. The highlanders focused on "their own business," both out of personal interest and obligation, as well as out of prudence, for they greatly valued privacy as well as autonomy and independence, and unwanted inquiries and intrusions into someone's activities could lead to retaliation (Liori 1991:82). The great commitment on the part of both men and women to their family and children rated public affairs as secondary, increasingly so as one moved from the close and immediate to the more distant, from the municipality, comune, to the Region of Sardinia, and beyond to Italy, Europe, and the world. Thus many events could take place which did not affect very directly the day-to-day life of most Sardinian highlanders.

Most Sardinian highlanders had a sense of great continuity; they lived in the towns of their ancestors, and these towns dated from many hundreds of years and even millennia. Strisaili, which later became Villagrande Strisaili, is found in tax records dating back to 1316 (Cocco 1986:233). Most highlanders had the same names as their ancestors of centuries previous. The family names of my Villagrande friends and acquaintances were the same as those recorded in Villagrande in 1744: Cannas, Melis, Rubiu, Demurtas, Seoni, Balloi, Cabiddu, Piras, Orru, Cabras, Congiu, Loi, etc.; and even full names were the same, with my landlord Antonio Cannas and his brother Pietro Cannas echoing namesakes of 1744 (Cocco 1986:242–43). Highland Sardinians were thus well rooted in place and in a long line of ancestors. There was among (at least some) rural Sardinians even a sense of communication with and assistance from the spirits of the ancestral dead (Zene 1996:10, note 12). Furthermore, highlanders often lived in the same houses (although in recent decades highly renovated and modernized) and used the same terraces, gardens, orchards, fields, and pastures as their ancestors of decades and centuries before. The established customs and practices of making a living and of "living" in general, known as *su connottu*, are rooted in the past and are sacralized as the spirit of the ancestors (Zene 1996:12).

There is no better example of continuity in the lives of the highlanders than the Roman Catholic Church, which has dominated and monopolized the spiritual life of Sardinians for over a millennium. Individuals' personal or "Christian" names were always saints' names, and individuals celebrated the birth dates of their saintly namesakes. The days were organized by Church rituals, and the days of the week were organized by the sabbath. Holidays throughout the year were holy-days, defined by the Church. Each town had its special patron saint and the birthday of the saint was the feast, *festa*, usually with elaborate entertainment, of the town's celebration of itself. Equally profound was the influence of the Church on such matters as family organization, succession, and inheritance, for Church law had structured many of the basic arrangements of daily life which highlanders took for granted.

MAKING A LIVING

Most Sardinian highlanders spent most of each day working for a living. For thousands of years, up to and well into the twentieth century, Ogliastrans and other Sardinian mountaineers lived by raising animals and growing plants, and by hunting and gathering natural species, to provide themselves with food and raw materials. Members of each household tried to produce everything needed for their own sustenance. Men, women, and children all participated in the diverse and labor-intensive productive activities, which were necessarily a central focus of daily attention and effort. While the nucleated town of small stone houses was the center of residence, often men were away at far-flung sheep stations months at a time, and during busy agricultural periods people stayed in distant fields and gardens. There were also terraced gardens near the houses and surrounding the towns which could be tended without staying away over night. So most highlanders of all sexes and ages spent their days arduously tending livestock, gardens, and agricultural crops, and travelling among the sites of these and between them and town. Much processing, such as cheese-making, crushing grapes for wine, and bread-baking, was done by hand, by human muscle power and sweat. So too with maintenance chores, such as bringing water to the house from the fountains, washing clothes in the river, and cutting and carrying firewood from the forest.

FAMILIES

For Sardinian highlanders, the primary point of reference was the nuclear family: parents and children, brothers and sisters. Each nuclear family formed a separate household, with its own separate dwelling. A new family was formed by a Church marriage and the relocation of the newly married couple to a residence of their own. In the past, marriages were almost always with members of the same community, the same agrotown, and the mates were chosen by the parents. Since World War II, young people date and choose their own spouses, increasingly from a wider population extending to other Sardinian communities, the Italian mainland, and even beyond. Often engagements last for ten years, while the two continue to live with their parents, saving for and building and furnishing a house of their own. Only when their own residence is ready and furnished, do they have their Church wedding—in some cases with their baby, born ahead of time, in attendance—and move in together.

The family in its household traditionally formed the working group that produced the necessities of life, as well as being a group of related consumers who lived together. Until recently, when school became truly obligatory, most children worked alongside of their parents, the boys in the fields or at the sheep station with their father, the girls in the garden and household with their mother. Everyone contributed to the family and everyone was supposed to have the interests of the family at heart. The individual's acts and qualities reflected on the family, and the family's qualities and standing reflected on the individual members. Sardinian highlanders usually took the view that, to use one of their own expressions, "the apple does not fall far from the tree"; that is, individuals tend to be like their families. The primary job of the man and woman, husband and wife, father and mother, was to bring children into the world and raise them well. Manhood meant providing for one's family; womanhood meant supporting and nurturing one's family in every way. "Duty" meant, above all, "family." Letting your family down was about the worst thing a person could do. People would sometimes complain about *sacrifici per i bambini*, "sacrifices for the children," but they were really bragging. Family members looked out for one another, stood together against outsiders, and kept their own family matters secret. The solidarity of the family was regularly manifested ritually, as in the obligatory presence of all available members for midday *pranzo*, the main meal of the day.

BEYOND THE NUCLEAR FAMILY

It would, however, be a mistake to see the nuclear family as an isolated monad, unattached to outsiders. Each parent of a family (the "family of procreation" as sociologists like to say) also was a member of another family, the one in which she or he grew up (the "family of orientation"). So each parent also had parents and uncles and aunts, and brothers and sisters, almost always living in the same community. These were the people to whom each parent continued to owe loyalty, and commonly felt strong affection. In practice this meant that each nuclear family (of procreation) had in the community a network of ongoing relationships with close kinsmen/women. Commonly those in the elder generation continued to help and support the families of their children, nieces and nephews. Reciprocal relations of cooperation and mutual aid, and sometimes formal partnerships in particular economic activities, were often established between members of the same generation, especially siblings, brothers and sisters. In other words, each small family had a network of kin, a kind of kinship safety net, ready to aid and support them as well as to call upon them for aid and support. This is where one turned for help with child care, care for the ill, labor tasks requiring many hands, defense against threats from the outside, and any other emergency.

Each individual also existed as part of and depended upon the larger community of the town and comune, within which she or he was recognized as an established resident with specified rights of membership, such as a voice in local governance and also access to communal resources, including house sites, water, firewood, pastures, agricultural land, and wild species of plants and animals. The community had traditionally also provided security against external threat to property and person, and continued in recent times to provide to a degree a safe refuge.

Community membership was manifested on social occasions such as the daily, early evening *passeggiata*, the public promenade or stroll on the main street and square (particularly popular with teenagers and young men and women) and ritual occasions such as the frequent and enthusiastically observed religious calendar and life cycle *feste*, feasts, which took place to celebrate the community patron saint's birthday, Christmas and Easter, and christenings and weddings. Community members were expected to be social, to show themselves in public and to socialize with their fellow townsmen and townswomen; solitary living and avoidance of others was disparaged and discouraged, and deemed a sign of illness. Traditionally women socialized with other women in their homes, in the neighborhood streets, at the fountain, and at the river where the clothes were washed, while men socialized with other men in the main town square, *piazza*, and in the bars, where they talked and played cards. Young people socialized during the public ritual of the passeggiata. All of this continued into the 1990s, although people's lives were not as much restricted to their own town.

Sardinian highlanders, however remote their towns may seem geographically and however remote their traditional life was from that of government offices and cities, have for centuries lived within larger social and political worlds. They have always had to deal with outsiders. Closest were the inhabitants of other towns in their regions, always seen as strangers, rivals, and potential enemies; although there was sometimes cordial visiting between towns during religious and life cycle feste. Out in the pastures, the shepherds had always to contend with the threat of rustlers from other towns (Caltagirone 1989). There were Sardinians from other regions, who might be acting in conjunction with or as agents for foreign powers. Throughout history there have been a series of foreign colonial governments imposing power through their soldiers, governors, feudal lords, and tax collectors. Since Sardinia fell under Italian control in 1861, Sardinians have had to deal with the Carabinieri, the branch of the military for internal security, the Guardia de Finanza, military agents of taxation, the Corpo Forestale, militarized forest rangers, and political party patrons bearing gifts in exchange for votes. Sardinian highlanders met the outsiders with considered mixes of resistance, avoidance, and obfuscation, but always with distrust and often with rejection.

It is noteworthy that Sardinian highland women, commonly somewhat more schooled than the men living in the pastures and thus more adept in writing and arithmetic, usually handled bureaucratic transactions with outsiders, and often did so in the 1990s. And it is the women,

generally speaking, who accepted without great reservation the presence in the community of priests, monks, nuns, and other Church officials who represented that great external power, the Roman Catholic
Church. The highland men tended to look much more diffidently at the
Church and its local representatives.

EVERYDAY LIFE AND NOTEWORTHY EVENTS

With this general appreciation of Sardinia and Sardinian highlanders established, I will turn to seven Sardinian events as I encountered them, in chronological order. But we must keep in mind that these
events arose within the stream of everyday life and were far from the
only concerns with which Sardinians were occupied or events that they
experienced. Consider the events we ourselves read about in our own
newspapers or hear reported on the radio or see on television. Events
that may seem monumental or devastating in themselves may stay with
us or may affect us little after we have put the paper down or turned off
the news report and returned to our everyday reality to live our own
lives. So too with particular highland Sardinians, even when they may
"belong" to some degree to the milieu of the events, they may not be
affected directly, and the indirect consequences for them might be very
mild within the larger context of their lives.

Continuing with the metaphor of the flow of daily life, the events
described below were, for particular highlanders, rather like the surface
waves, or the sidewash, hardly interfering with the overall flow. But for
other individuals who were affected directly, the events were in some cases
like rampaging floods that transformed the flow of their lives. I want to
make it clear that all highland Sardinians were not at all times swept
away by events such as the ones I describe below. Nor were those who were
greatly affected by one event necessarily greatly affected by the next.

Furthermore, these events did not happen all at once. Rather, by my
observations, they occurred in sequence. This struck me very strongly. In
any one six-month period, Ogliastrini and sometimes all highlanders or
all Sardinians, were thinking and talking and writing and meeting about
one particular event or issue or crisis. In a way, the event or issue seemed
to define public life. But the domination of the event or issue was always
limited. After six months or a year, some other, totally different event or
issue dominated people's minds and public discourse. The year after, it
was yet another event or crisis, this one too quite different from the previous ones. The tenor of each moment, of each period, was shaped by the
particular event dominant at that time.

So, we must not think that Sardinian highlanders were coping with all of these events at once, or that their lives were made up of crises on all sides. But it is true that many of these events—kidnappings, government intrusions, murders, droughts, job schemes, bombings—were manifestations of ongoing processes of the environment and society of highland Sardinia, as I shall try to explain when I examine each particular event. These underlying processes were not always manifest in the current events of every week, month, or year; instead, for periods they remained latent in ongoing relations and activities, but always with the potential, and likelihood, of arising in new events. Fortunately for, or perhaps because of, the sanity of the highlanders, events tended to happen, or were recognized and noted and responded to, one by one.

DROUGHT, 1987–88

For cultivators and shepherds of the Mediterranean region, where precipitation is modest at best, and comes mostly in the winter and seldom in the hot summer, water is life. Where people depend on precipitation rather than irrigation—and almost all Sardinian agriculture depends on rainfall rather than irrigation—agricultural production lives or dies by rain- and snowfall. All cultivated plants require water and all grazing and browsing livestock require natural pasture. A year of maximum precipitation brings bumper crops of grain, vegetables, and fruit, fine pasture, many lambs, kids, and calves, much milk, and many cheeses. Without good rainfall, crops and pastures are poor, and livestock produces less offspring, milk, and meat. Poor crops and less animal products mean low income, and low income means a decline in standard of living, perhaps a halt to building, education, and reproduction, and even a decline in health.

During the two years 1987–88, there was a drought in Sardinia and Ogliastra. Rainfall in 1987–88 was respectively at 299 mm and 340.2 mm (ISTAT 1991:26), well below the Sardinian average of 448.75 mm, or 17.67 inches (ISTAT 1986:7), which is itself one of the lowest levels of precipitation in Italy. Good years see much more precipitation, such as 1985 with 623.4 mm; and really bad years can be somewhat worse, such as 1981 with 236.8 mm. But to the Ogliastrini, the two-year drought of 1987–88 was quite bad enough. Crops were down or failing and milk was low. Two years in a row! Everyone was worried and everyone was scrambling.

For several thousand years until the second half of the nineteenth century, Ogliastrini and other Sardinian highlanders lived by consuming the things that they themselves produced. The household was the unit of production and consumption, and all family members, including children, contributed their labor. Sardinian mountaineers were *subsistence* producers and did not exchange or sell much. In each highland comune, municipality, most every family had an *orto*, garden, and grew vegetables and fruit, and vines, and olive, almond, and fruit trees. In some comuni, every family grew wheat in more distant fields and also had a small flock of sheep and goats. In other comuni, some families specialized in growing wheat, and were called *contadini*, cultivators, and others specialized in raising sheep and goats and were called *pastori*, shepherds; within these communities, wheat was traded for cheese and meat.

The pastori grazed their sheep and goats on uncultivated, natural pasture, sometimes burning off scrub *macchia* and even oak forest to expand the natural pasture. To provide both moderate temperature and the best pasture for their flocks, the shepherds migrated seasonally between the coastal lowlands, mild during the winter, and the mountains, mild during the summer, thus avoiding the scorching lowland summer and the freezing mountain winter. Each shepherd had an established sheep station, *ovile*, in the mountains, and some shepherds had them in the lowlands as well. This *transhumance* between lowland and highland sheep stations kept shepherds away from their town for a good part of the year.

The shepherds had plenty to contend with, for beyond the many complex aspects of herding and husbanding livestock, and the delicate endeavor of making superb sheep's and goat's milk cheese, they had to defend their flocks against predation from rustlers, abusive grazers, and violent opponents. In the huge and open landscape of the pastures, the customary law was that of *noi pastori*, we (the community of) shepherds. Stealing sheep from flocks of other communities was an accepted form of virility display, entrepreneurship, and sport (Caltagirone 1989). From the physical exertion of handling livestock, shepherds became strong men with mighty forearms and "hands like hams"; from the challenge of competition and threat, they became hard men, ready to act, violently if necessary, to respond to an *offesa*, an attack on a flock and thus an offense against the shepherd's honor and standing.

The primary responsibility of a shepherd, the male head, *padrone*, of his household, was the family flock. Whether the shepherd was away in the pasture or temporarily back in town, the female head, *padrona*, took primary responsibility for cultivating the garden crops, running the household, controlling the money, maintaining social ties, and dealing with officials. Life in highland Sardinian comuni thus had two contrasting and complementary sides, each with its own locales, activities, and orientations (Edelsward 1988:4):

Noi Pastori	*The Town*
male	female
nature	culture
livestock	garden
pasture/wilderness	home
movement	stability
hardships	comfort
isolation	society
independence	responsibility
competition	cooperation
conflict	control
enemies/friends	family and kin
vulnerability	security
suspicion	trust
atomism	mutual aid
protect/lose sheep	protect/lose face

The town itself also palely reflected the two sides, with houses and neighborhoods allocated to women, and bars and *piazze*, squares, allocated to men, with neither women nor men expected to loiter in the sphere of the other.

Beginning in the latter part of the nineteenth century, a market in sheep's and goat's milk opened, responding to the demand from continental Italy and from Italian immigrants in North and South America. The Romano Company and other commercial dairies opened in Sardinia, and Sardinian shepherds sold them some or all of their milk. Shepherds thus started producing milk not only for their own consumption but also to sell for money. This commercial demand, together with a decline in grain cultivation resulting from the import of cheap American grain, led to a great expansion in pastoralism, and in the number of sheep and goats in Sardinia. Increasing in consequence were the incomes and standard of living of shepherds and their families, and of the highland communities as a whole. After World War II, Sardinian highland communities got electricity, piped water, and motor vehicles, and there was a great investment in new houses and high-quality furniture.

The drought of 1987–88, leaving the pastures brown and livestock udders dry, the garden crops unwatered, and the vines and orchards thirsty, threatened the income of Ogliastrini and other highland Sardinians. Shepherds had to maintain their increased capital costs, such as the vehicles they used to go between the town and the pastures, to buy expensive feed to maintain their animals, and to buy food that their gardens were not providing. The many Ogliastrini who worked in other sectors also suffered from the failure of garden crops and the decline in availability of local cheese and meat. The drought lowered income, raised costs, enforced a bridled standard of living, and led to gloom, frayed nerves, and touchiness among Ogliastrini and other highlanders.

Most seriously, the drought and its economic consequences discouraged young people from continuing with and especially from initiating careers in agriculture or animal husbandry. Ogliastrini would sigh, and say, *"Non rende,"* "It doesn't pay." In this way the drought reinforced the widely held, contemporary view that any work, such as agriculture, without a secure salary, without a guaranteed income, was greatly inferior to hard-to-get *posti fissi*, permanent posts, either in government service or in a labor union dominated industry. Private and independent workers, whether shepherds, agriculturalists, artisans, or small-scale entrepreneurs, were, it was said, at the mercy of droughts, depressions, and fluctuations in the market. They were ever vulnerable to changing conditions which could destroy their incomes and security, unlike occupants of permanent posts whose work and retirement income were guaranteed and who could enjoy security with a sure serenity. These sentiments were reinforced by the appreciation that this particular drought was not a unique accident, but an inevitable event in a repeating climatic cycle. Just as in the past, such as 1981–83, there had been bad droughts, so the drought of 1987–88 would inevitably be followed in four, five, or six years or so by another bad drought and its disastrous economic consequences.

However, the search for a *posto fisso*, permanent post, was not necessarily a rational selection among available alternatives, as it might initially appear and as the young Sardinians usually thought of it. For the enthroning of the permanent post as an ideal of employment succeeded not only in demeaning the main, existing local job possibilities, that is, agriculture and animal husbandry, which drew on existing natural resources as well as established local knowledge and skills; at the same time, it celebrated and set as an employment goal something that was not commonly available in Ogliastra and Barbagia: permanent, secure jobs with large organizations. In other words, the droughts, among other influences, drove people to reject the imperfect possible for the perfect impossible, leaving most of those Ogliastrini who set their hearts on permanent posts permanently disappointed and frustrated (Edelsward 1995; Assmuth 1997). I knew a young shepherd in Villagrande who, although he loved the animals and loved his work, quit shepherding in 1993 under pressure from his young wife to find more secure employment. He was very fortunate, after two years of waiting and doing informal (black-market) construction work, to end up with a permanent, but only half-time, position on a government-funded reforestation scheme (discussed later in this chapter).

For the shepherds and cultivators facing the drought and reeling under their losses and fears, there were more immediate expedients to which they turned. For now, unlike centuries and millennia in the past, they were not entirely on their own, forced to suffer their misfortunes as best they could. This being 1987–88 and the temporal pinnacle of the Italian welfare state, as well as a moment of burgeoning European Economic Community (EEC, and since November 1993 known as the European Union) intervention, Sardinians could turn for aid to government agencies. Through this period, Sardinia and the Mezzogiorno, the south of Italy, received many transfer payments from the central government in Rome. Economically marginal regions of Europe received payments from the EEC for infrastructure projects (such as corrals, stalls, watering troughs) and production subsidies (for raising more or raising less of a crop or more or fewer livestock). By the time of the drought, Highland Sardinians had come to depend on government *contributi*, subsidies, such as a Sardinian Regional subsidy to support prices for sheep's milk. In response to the losses of the drought, the Sardinian Regional government offered drought compensation payments to shepherds and cultivators. So in the towns of Ogliastra and other regions of Sardinia, padrone, women household heads, determinedly searched out the proper government forms, figured out what information was needed, constructed and collected the information, prepared the documentation (always extensive in Italy), and submitted the applications. Payments arrived and to a degree compensated for the losses and alleviated the crisis. But the sense of insecurity remained. Wet years in 1989–92 followed the drought, and compensation payments stopped. Cultivators and shepherds were glad to see the land green again and their crops and animals fruitful, but they still shook their heads, wondering how they were going to do without their drought compensation payments.

VENDETTA, 1990–91

The news was like a blow to the stomach for Villagrandesi. Antonio Lotto had been ambushed, shot, and killed while driving back to Villagrande from his highland sheep-station in Villagrande territory (*L'Unione Sarda,* 29 Sept. 1990:22). Although this murder sickened Villagrandesi, it did not entirely surprise them. During the previous year, both Antonio and his brother Mario had been ambushed, but had escaped. Antonio and his brothers were directly engaged in a vendetta with several other shepherds, and this was not the first death. Another brother, Salvatore, had publicly shot and killed another shepherd, whom he believed had repeatedly committed grave *offese* against his flock, his and his family's interests, and consequently his honor and manhood. The murder of Antonio was in response to the previous murder by his brother.

The safety and security of Ogliastrini, Barbacini, and other Sardinian highlanders, especially for those who work far out in the fields and pastures and stay away from the towns, rests largely in their own hands. Right up to the mid-1990s no authority closely supervised day-to-day activities in the Sardinian mountains. Men were largely left to protect themselves and their property. The Italian state, the only central agency of social control and coercion, did not, due to difficulties of travel, transportation, communication, and cost, effectively reach into the countryside. This left people to protect themselves through *self-help*—action by the injured against the injurer. There were no collective defense groups based on kinship, territory, or association, primarily because the state, which always claims a monopoly on the right of coercion, suppressed independent coercive agencies, such as local security groups, as threats to itself. So it was left to the individual to engage in retaliation for any attack, to respond to any offense.

Sardinian highland countrymen arm themselves (discretely to avoid the eyes of the state) in order to defend themselves and to answer attacks. They must act on their own with *balentia*, courage, skill, and astuteness, and be capable of resolving even the riskiest situation. When people act on disagreements, attacking and destroying life or property, this is an offesa that requires retaliation and becomes a vendetta. In highland Sardinia, pursuing a vendetta is mandatory, a duty. "In Barbagia, someone who does not take vengeance, is not a man. To an attack, one responds with a reaction equal and contrary. For serious offenses, a vendetta would be implacable" (Liori 1991:103).

Highlanders are very aware that offending someone, damaging someone's property, or injuring someone's person or reputation can lead to swift retaliation and brutal retribution. Such a response acts as a deterrence to offending others, and leads people to measure their words and actions carefully, mindful of possible consequences (Liori 1991:103). In the event of damage, injury, or loss of life, fellow community members beyond the protagonists involved in the vendetta or *faida*, feud, tend to be passive, even withdrawn. The highland rule, expressed in Sardinian as *negare ferru ferru*, is to mind your own business and keep silent (Liori 1991:82). As the old World War II poster puts it, "loose tongues lose lives."

Balentia, vendetta, faida, and silence are the law of the highlands (Pigliaru 1975) that have for millennia structured conflict and served to impose an order of balanced opposition and fear, producing a kind of "ordered anarchy" (Evans-Pritchard 1940). Yet beyond this highland field of ordered anarchy have distantly hovered imperial, colonial, and state authorities, ready to intervene, frequently clumsily and ineffectually, if highland conflict impinged upon their interests. The growth of the modern state in the nineteenth and twentieth centuries led to a more ambitious attempt by Italian state authorities to impose effective state control throughout and insure that state laws and procedures were paramount. Increased interventions by state authorities and their enforcement agencies, as in the establishment of military Carabinieri stations in all towns, has not been received by all Ogliastrini and other highlanders with great enthusiasm, nor has the determined and systematic campaign of the Carabinieri to disarm highlanders. Resistance to the imposition by Rome of "foreign" law and enforcement, as it is seen by some Sardinians, takes the standard form of social isolation of members of the Carabinieri (Liori 1991:37–38) and the frequent and repeated shooting and bombings of Carabinieri stations, cars, homes, and even individuals, at least one of which happens every day in Sardinia (*L'Unione Sarda*, passim):

> Orgosolo, Gavoi and Ploaghe: Three Attacks on the Carabinieri (4 March 1991:11)

> At Escalaplano, A Bomb [thrown at] the Car of a Carabiniere, It's the Fifth Attack (30 June 1991:24)

> Targets in Uniform: A Policeman Wounded at Orune, at Oliena the Carabinieri Are Still in the Gun Sight (3 January 1992:18)

Even municipal, comune officials, such as mayors and council members, who serve as the lowest tier in the state administration as well as representatives of the local population, have been repeatedly subject to threats, shooting, and bombings as members of the local population express their dissent through violent self-help.

The murder of Antonio Lotto in September 1990 was an event in a vendetta cycle, and not many Villagrandesi or Ogliastrini would have been so sanguine as to say that this particular vendetta was closed or that the time of vendetta was over. When in November 1991, Giuseppe Rubiu, leaving his Villagrande house early in the morning on his way to his sheep-station for first milking, was killed by two shotgun blasts, some Villagrandesi wondered if this was not retribution for the death of Antonio Lotto.

These sad events were a reminder, if a reminder were needed, that traditional Sardinian highland mores and norms continued in force in some quarters, and that there had been no resolution of the contradiction between local customary law with the centralized legal institutions of the Italian state, deemed by some highlanders, if a minority, to be an occupying foreign power, and by many highlanders to be clumsy, insensitive to local needs, and too far away ever to be anything else.

THE STRUGGLE AGAINST THE
NATIONAL PARK, 1991–92

Enabling legislation for the Gennargentu National Park, originally suggested in 1958 (Scuola 1992:279) and formally proposed in 1962 (Natali 1992:36), which foresaw a final agreement between the Italian national government and the regional government of Sardinia for the permanent establishment of the park, was passed on 6 December 1991 by the Italian parliament in Rome (Murgia 1992:42). This huge national park, named after the major mountain range at its center, would encompass 59,000 hectares in fourteen comuni, their towns and territories, of the central highlands of Sardinia, including those of Ogliastra (Scuola 1992:293). The establishment of the park, once finalized, would effectively bring local municipalities, their communities and territories, under the direct control of national and regional park authorities. This was viewed by the majority of highlanders of Ogliastra and Barbagia as no less than the usurpation of their property and the violation of their rights as local inhabitants. They felt that the establishment of this park was a further step in their subjection by distant agents of the state. They were incensed by the arrogance and intrusiveness of the park initiative and vowed to oppose the park and defend their rights.

Villagrandesi and the inhabitants of each of the highland comuni believed that they themselves owned their comune, its town, territory, and all of its resources, and that it was theirs to do with what they would. They and their ancestors—they would tell you—have lived in their comune since time immemorial, building the town and the terraces and the country dwellings, and drawing on and husbanding the natural resources. The current inhabitants argued that they have *usi civici*, rights as members of the community to the resources of their territory, rights which have been established and validated over the centuries. (For these views in the Ogliastran mountain comune of Baunei, see Heatherington 1993.) These rights included free access to the common lands which made up a large part of the territory in the comune. The inhabitants had an established right to graze their sheep, goats, cattle, horses, and pigs; to build sheep stations, including huts, sheds, and corrals, as bases for their flocks and as the locales for cheese-making; to draw water from natural water sources such as springs and streams; to collect wild plants, such as mushrooms and berries, and seeds, such as acorns; to hunt wild animals, such as game birds and wild boar; to fish in the lakes and streams; to cut down trees for firewood, the main heating fuel; to enter and leave at will, using the forests, mountains, and lakes for recreation and enjoyment, such as walks, picnics, exercise, and assignations. These rights, it was believed, were inherent in formal membership, *residenza*, in each community.

Proposers of the Gennargentu National Park, members of both regional and national governments, and their active and sometimes vociferous allies in the environmental movement, such as the World Wildlife Fund, saw central Sardinia and its vast Gennargentu zone as one of the last, untouched areas of pristine natural wilderness remaining in Italy and Europe. The human population density is one of the lowest in Europe and the area abounds in rare and beautiful plants, animals, and landscapes. They felt that this zone had to be preserved as a rare remnant of natural patrimony for the broader edification and welfare of Sardinia, Italy, Europe, and humanity at large (e.g., Camarda 1992). The establishment of the park would guarantee the preservation of this rare resource by placing it under the control and supervision of publicly minded officials and environmental experts. The entire Gennargentu zone would be protected from use and exploitation that would degrade the environment and ruin its pristine character. The Gennargentu Park would thus, it was alleged, be a great step forward for civilized environmentalism.

The tens of thousands of highland Sardinians whose comuni made up the Gennargentu area—Villagrande alone has four thousand residents— rejected the conceptual annihilation that they suffer when their territories are characterized as unoccupied "wilderness" primarily significant for its wild plants and animals and landscape. As the highlanders did not hesitate to say, the farthest reaches of these Gennargentu municipal territories, including the slopes of Gennargentu mountain itself, have been used by their ancestors for millennia for collecting natural plants and hunting wild animals, for raising sheep and goats, and for cultivation. This so-called uninhabited wilderness was anything but that; every peak, every valley, every spot was known, named, and used by its highland inhabitants.

The establishment of a national park on community territories, which would define residents as intruders and potential destroyers, threatened their established rights, their livelihoods, and their identities. The inhabitants scoffed at the idea that the land and forests and animals in their territories had to be protected from them. After all, they would ask, was it not they who have conserved their territories over the millennia, while those from Cagliari and Rome, who wished to establish the park because of the "pristine" environment, have exploited, degraded, and destroyed their own environments? The highlanders, threatened by the park with expropriation and exclusion from their own territories, asked wonderingly why their territories should be frozen in time and made into an "ecological zoo" to benefit the sensibilities and sensations of urbanites in Cagliari, Rome, and Milan who wanted to don shorts and bush jackets and wander the wilderness for vacations. And, in the usual Sardinian highland spirit of resistance, anti-park graffiti appeared on walls throughout the highland towns; the following are from Villagrande:

> SI ALLA PASTORIZIA
> NO AL PARCO
> Yes to [livestock] pastoralism.
> No to the park.

> NO AL PARCO TRUFFA
> No to the park swindle.

> NO AL PARCO
> PERCHÉ CI DEVONO SFRUTTARE I ROMANI?
> SIAMO COSÌ FESSI?
> No to the park.
> Why must the Romans exploit us?
> Are we such suckers?

In addition, various highlanders were warning, and some threatening—not notices to be taken lightly from highland Sardinians—that the creation of the park would be resisted with bullets, fire, and bombs.

Government initiatives to establish the Gennargentu National Park were by no means the first external interventions in controlling local environments in the central highlands. Conservation of the remaining oak forests, along with preserving the coastal beaches, had been a focus of Italian and Sardinian environmental activists and, more significantly, the regional government of Sardinia. Concerned, for example, about the destructive effects of herding in the forests, regional regulations have forbidden the herding of goats and restricted the herding of sheep in the forests. Substantive counter-arguments of knowledgeable shepherds—for example that the grazing of flocks in forests reduces the likelihood of forest fires because the animals consume the undergrowth of grasses that when dry are highly combustible and can catch fire—have been ignored in favor of the views of outside "experts."

Similarly, concern about the cutting of oak trees to supply the highland towns with firewood, their traditional form of energy for cooking and heating, led to the imposition of regional government regulations limiting the period of cutting and the number and choice of trees to be cut. The delay in 1991 of regional government permission to begin cutting the firewood in Baunei, another Ogliastran mountain town, led to the "firewood rebellion," with local residents occupying the municipal offices, demonstrating in the streets, and blocking the Orientale, the main eastern highway of Sardinia that runs through the town. To the reader accustomed to the convenience and low cost of oil or electric heating, or unfamiliar with the damp, freezing winters of Mediterranean highlands, the obsession of highland Sardinians with firewood might seem excessive. But having lived through two chilling highland winters, and having balked at the truly outrageous Italian prices of electricity, oil, and gas, I can confirm that it is difficult to be environmentally "green" when one is blue with cold. Like everyone else in Villagrande, I ordered my load of oak firewood and huddled in front of the fireplace to keep warm. And, following the lead of Villagrande men, I roasted fresh meat in the intensely preferred local fashion, over an oak wood fire.

Lack of observation of forest regulations by local residents led to the establishment and diffusion throughout the region of an enforcement agency, the Corpo Forestale, Forest Rangers, to police the forests. Local resistance in the highlands and elsewhere to the rangers led, in typical Italian government fashion, to militarization of the rangers, who were decked out with uniforms, weapons, and overland vehicles. In the highland communities where they were stationed, they were viewed by many highlanders as external agents coercively enforcing foreign laws, much the same as the Carabinieri, and were treated by local residents as unwelcome occupiers (Heatherington 1993:ch. VI).

It was no accident that the launching of the national park followed the banning of livestock from the forests and the imposition of controls on the exploitation of the forests. These events, and the reactions to them—the "firewood rebellion" in Baunei and the anti-park graffiti, meetings, declarations, and demonstrations that swept the highland communities—were part of an ongoing trend of increasing government control over local environments and the nullification, suspension, or restriction of local rights and powers over the local environment and its resources. Furthermore, this illegal power grab, or "enlightened intervention," depending upon one's perspective, was itself part of a larger trend of more intrusive and more effective government control, especially in regard to possession of arms, payment of taxes, and regulation of spatial movement, all increasingly scrutinized by state enforcement agencies such as the Carabinieri and Guardia di Finanza. Sardinian highlanders observed this trend, and many did not like it. Each event was, to many, like another blow. Some spoke of striking back violently. Others spoke hopefully of a new trend of regional decentralization within the EEC, of the EEC as a confederation of regions and peoples, with the national states fading away, a hope shared by regionalists in Lombardia, Venezia, and elsewhere in the Italian north, and in Corsica, Catalonia, and elsewhere in the Mediterranean. But in the meantime, the highlanders were girding their loins in anticipation of new events manifesting the increasing intrusiveness of the regional and national governments.

THE BOMBING, 1993

On 30 June, 1993, "Plant M," one of the few modern production facilities owned and run by Villagrandesi in Villagrande territory, was bombed by unknown assailants, resulting in total destruction of the current inventory and serious damage to the infrastructure. This was a devastating blow to the small cooperative that had struggled to design, found, finance, and build the company and which had with some difficulty managed to establish viable production procedures, organize labor, begin production, find customers, sell their product, and meet costs while paying back loans. After the bomb, production was completely halted, and the plant went out of operation while the directors tried to stay loan payments and to find the resources necessary to get back into production. In June 1998, five years later, the plant had not yet gone back into production, although the operators still hoped to get it started again.

A bomb, by damaging, communicated a message, and the language of damage was well known to highland Sardinians. It was the language spoken by those engaged in self-help, in the correction of offenses and attacks. It was a way in which public opinion manifested itself, although the extent to which any particular act of self-help represented majority opinion could be a matter of debate. But whether or not representative of broader public opinion in Villagrande, what exactly was the message conveyed by the bombing?

While the authors of the bombing of Plant M were unknown, and those running the plant were devastated, the bombing itself surprised no one in Villagrande, including the members of the plant cooperative. Villagrandesi saw this bombing as an expression of *invidia*, envy, at the establishment of Plant M and an acting out of resentment against the plant and the people associated with it. The bombing of the plant was by no means an original or unique event; on the contrary, it was seen as one of many diverse expressions of envy. For invidia was regarded by all Villagrandesi as a powerful force in the life of the community. Any unusual or exceptional accomplishment or achievement on the part of anyone in Villagrande would lead, on the part of other Villagrandesi, to criticism, resentment, obstruction, resistance, and, ultimately, destruction. Many Villagrandesi and ex-Villagrandesi complained of this and all acknowledged it.

Villagrandese school girls complained that dressing a bit differently brought negative comments from peers; college students objected that gaining a higher education made them targets of criticism and belittling; professionals said that their achievements brought backbiting and attempts at undermining them; entrepreneurs establishing businesses in Villagrande faced not only daunting economic odds and competition, but attacks on their very efforts to succeed; and provincial or regional politicians lamented that their fellow Villagrandesi would vote against them rather than see them gain or continue in high office. Any effort beyond the ordinary, any achievement beyond the average, any outstanding accomplishment—whether personal, social, educational, economic, or political—became in Villagrande a target for attack. Community members could not stand the greater success of one of its members and would attempt to undercut that success.

The widespread presence of envy in Villagrande and other Sardinian communities can be understood not as a psychological characteristic of idiosyncratic individuals, of twisted minds, but rather as a shared propensity, characteristic of, and inculcated by local culture. That is, beliefs and values of the local culture encouraged and supported envy, a reaction of resentment and rejection against those who rose above others. If we consider envy, which is a way of speaking about the emotion that individuals have, as a more general social phenomenon, we can see that it is a *leveling mechanism*, a social process that rejects actions and their concrete manifestations which raise a person above others in the community. That is, envy polices and defends equality in the community, insuring that community members remain more or less the same status.

This equality, in turn, reinforces community solidarity and town membership as a focus of identity, upon which the strong local patriotism, *campanilismo*, of highland communities is based. Being equal means being equivalent members of the community, the commonalities of community members outweighing their differences. Inequality, which could arise from different degrees of individual accomplishment, undermines this equivalence and thus undermines community solidarity. Many Villagrandesi, including young people who had gone away to school and university, had a strong commitment to living in Villagrande and to Villagrande as a strong community, because it was very important to them that they were known, that they belonged, that they had a place in the community. These people were likely to be sympathetic to the needs of the community, to the ideal equality of its members, and to community solidarity, and to be less supportive of individualistic striving.

Many Villagrandesi who were strongly oriented to personal achievement and who saw the envy of the community smothering all striving, left Villagrande, migrating to the more open coastal towns or to the cities, rather than struggling against the resistance of their fellow community members. Jobs and opportunities were limited in highland Sardinia, so, for people with entrepreneurial or professional aspirations, leaving the constraints of the highland communities and moving to the areas of opportunity was a unified, if not painless, shift. Ironically, Villagrandesi who left the town and gained success outside, at the expense of outsiders, were lauded and feted in their abandoned home community. Those who stayed and pursued their projects, like the founders of Plant M, had to be very tough, smart, and probably lucky in order to deal with the local opposition and to succeed at their initiatives.

The founders of Plant M knew that many Villagrandesi resented their project. Some community members had been heard to complain that large government subsidies had been obtained by the founders of the plant and that everyone knew that government aid came only through corruption. It was true that there had been government subsidies of various kinds; such a large undertaking on the part of ordinary highlanders would hardly have been possible otherwise. The plant founders, for their part, complained bitterly about the inordinate delays and perverse difficulties of gaining government support and the various ways that they had been left "holding the bag" for the project—for example, having to begin paying off loans before government permits arrived to allow the plant to begin operating. The founders, a number of whom were relatives, believed that envy about the plant was intensified because their family, previously successful at other, more conventional enterprises, was already the subject of envy. There was the feeling among many people in the community that families succeeded unusually well only at the expense of other families—an idea known in the anthropological literature as *the image of the limited good* (Foster 1965). The plant founders felt that the establishment of the plant, on top of previous accomplishments of their family, had been more than some community members could tolerate and that this had led to the bombing of the plant. They wondered if members of a less prominent family might have been allowed the initiative of the plant without such dire retaliation.

A number of educated "modernists" and professional and entrepreneurial strivers from Villagrande and other highland towns, and also observers of the highland scene from more distant seats in Sardinian regional government, universities, and media, criticized the cultural complex of envy, equality, and solidarity. They used a modernist discourse approbating modernity, progress, and development. These critics of the closed, egalitarian, highland communities argued that when innovation is discouraged and change is suppressed, progress is impossible and stagnation is the result. This argument carried weight with highland Sardinians, because highlanders knew that their high standard of living and the availability of good, secure posts, posti fissi, depended at least to a degree upon "progress" and further change, and virtually no one was ready to return to the pre-war days of endless backbreaking labor, of *miseria*, poverty, and of subsistence insecurity. Nor did highlanders want to see their towns shrink and die from a hemorrhage of their sons and daughters seeking jobs in coastal towns, cities, and on the mainland.

The bombs in Villagrande and other highland towns spoke out for equality, solidarity, and continuity in the community and against individualistic striving, inequality, and change. The message of the bombs was opposition to the discourse and implementation of modernization, progress, and development. The bombs expressed powerfully the reservations of many highlanders about the erosion of community values and identity. But the bombs did not express the ambivalence that the majority of highlanders felt as they tried to reconcile the often incompatible community values and the recently won and much cherished modern standard of living.

THE ALLOCATION OF GOVERNMENT JOBS, 1993

After years of political lobbying, government planning, and highland hoping, in 1993 an Italian government reforestation scheme (*rimboscamento*, from *bosco*, forest), was put into place in Villagrande, following similar schemes in some other highland towns. This reforestation scheme was part of a broader environmental effort in Sardinia to replant areas, mountainsides especially, that had been denuded of trees over the centuries through lumbering, fires, or clearance for pasture. Among the many possible benefits envisaged from renewed forests were halting of erosion, increase of wildlife, use of inland areas for tourism, and limited commercial offtake of lumber.

Villagrandesi were ecstatic about the reforestation scheme. It was not so much that they were ecstatic about the environmental renewal, about the new forests fighting erosion, or about the projected arrival of more rodents, birds, and ruminants, although some Villagrandesi favored the idea. Rather, they were ecstatic because this scheme provided sixty well-paying, full-time, permanent, government jobs, with full benefits, including permanent tenure and generous pensions. All sixty jobs would go to Villagrande residents, if not to every individual, then to fathers, brothers, sisters, husbands, wives, daughters, or sons. This was a large number of new jobs in a community of four thousand people, and their arrival was even more impressive because posti fissi were so rare in highland towns and in all of Ogliastra. And by the time this scheme was put into place, the transformation of the Italian political system was well under way, as were austerity measures initiated by the Italian government to meet European Union criteria for joining the common currency. It was becoming clear, even to distant observers in the Sardinian highlands, that employment schemes and new government jobs were about to become a thing of the past. The rimboscamento scheme was one of the last jewels to fall from the withering hand of the corpse of the old regime. Villagrandesi rejoiced in this gift, come finally to them before the corpse was interred and the new, more austere hands sealed the government coffers.

Villagrandesi rejoiced the arrival of the jobs, and then feared the consequences. One major problem was that those parts of the communal land to be reforested were currently occupied by sheep stations and used for pastures. How could the shepherds be turned off the land and turned away from their livings? It was decided that the shepherds who gave up their sheep stations must be guaranteed jobs on the reforestation scheme. Yes, but what about the shepherds' sons and their lost opportunities to become shepherds? They too, it was decided, must be guaranteed jobs. But wait, said others, some of those shepherds' sons had no intention of becoming shepherds, and now they are getting jobs that we might have had. And so the discussion went.

Another major problem was the fear among Villagrandesi that the sixty jobs would be allocated by members of the Municipal Council to their own relatives and friends rather than fairly throughout the community. This kind of mistrust resulted from the almost universal assumption in Villagrande and throughout Sardinia and Italy that favoritism was the basis of all public decisions and all allocation of benefits. It was almost always assumed, for example, that someone could not gain a job through merit alone, but only through connections, and that any official could be influenced or bought, if the mediator, whether a relative, political or church official, or businessman or -woman, were powerful enough or the bribe large enough.

The public culture of Italy was one of mistrust, and, partly in defense, the modus operandi was *arrangiare*, to resolve one's problems however possible, such as through special agreements with others. Almost always in Italy, there was a legal and official, and often virtually impossible way to do something, and then there was the practical and effective way to do it. In decision making, Sardinians and Italians, bureaucrats included, usually preferred to look at individual cases and situations rather than general rules and laws. This resulted in considerable flexibility, for good or ill, and sometimes considerable humanity, especially for visiting anthropologists and other ignorant and harmless guests. However, this practice also resulted in substantial uncertainty and a consequent sense of insecurity in the minds of any Sardinian or Italian needing a decision or help. This was one of the reasons that, as a general life strategy, the search for security was such a high priority for Sardinians.

When the time came for the sixty rimboscamento jobs to be allocated, Villagrandesi job seekers and their relatives had worked themselves into a frenzy of anxiety, and their representations and importunities to the authorities involved in the hiring became increasingly frantic and menacing. Members of the Villagrande Municipal Council, responsible for allocating the posts under the watchful eye of regional administrative and judicial officials, became ever more worried not just about accusations of favoritism, but about bombings and other violent reprisals on the municipal offices and on members of the council by disgruntled applicants who did not win posts. In response to this overwhelming pressure, the council decided to spread the benefits more widely than originally planned. Thus, they split the sixty full-time jobs into 120 half-time jobs; one group of sixty workers would work for six months of the year and then be replaced by a second group who worked during the other six-month period. This enabled the council to provide benefits to twice as many people. In fact, this arrangement was even better than the full-time posts, for, after two years of work, the employees would be eligible for unemployment payments worth about 50 percent of their pay during the six months when they were not working. Thus the total flowing to Villagrandesi would be the equivalent of sixty full-time jobs *plus* 50 percent more in unemployment payments.

The result of this decision was that many of the Villagrandesi seeking jobs got them. Furthermore, many of the shepherds could work a rimboscamento job and retain their flocks. Of all of the shepherds who lost their sheep stations and pasture areas to reforestation and who thus received jobs on the scheme, only one gave up his flock. The others all kept their flocks for both the activity and the supplementary income, and entered into partnerships to allow maintenance of the flocks. During the six months away from reforestation, the men would return to shepherding, covering for partners who were on their six months of work in reforestation. Then the partners would switch. Because the Villagrandesi were not totally confident that the "guaranteed" reforestation jobs would not be cancelled by the government, if that suited its purposes, they wanted some economic security in case they had to fall back on their own resources. To provide themselves with this insurance, Villagrande shepherds thought it was a good idea to hang onto their flocks and their shepherding.

Of course, not everyone was happy. Some who had been confident of getting full-time jobs now found themselves with a lesser arrangement. Others in the community, themselves working full time in the private sector, felt that the jobs and unemployment payments were very generous for those who got them, but that it was they themselves and other workers who had to pay the taxes to support the reforestation jobs and the additional unemployment payments. As well, some self-styled progressive Villagrandesi who had seen in the reforestation scheme the end of pastoralism and the end of shepherding as a significant occupation, and who applauded this advancement beyond the archaic shepherding mode of life and its associated customs, were disappointed when shepherding continued without much loss of strength.

FOREST FIRES, 1994

During the summer of 1994, fires could be seen throughout central Sardinia, on the slopes of mountains and here and there in the valleys. Natural pastures were aflame, and forests were burning. The fires were being battled by the *anti-incendi* squads, easily visible in their orange-colored, presumably fire-retardant, overalls. These fire-fighting squads which, by 1994, used fleets of tank trucks and formations of water-dumping helicopters, had been formalized and professionalized over the previous decade. But estimates put the summer losses at 65,000 hectares. Irreplaceable forests of old oak had been reduced to carbonated hulks and dead ashes. New forests, recently planted by the reforestation scheme, were wiped to the ground. Orchards, vineyards, and fields were lost, and some houses too. Every highland comune was hit; almost every community had serious losses to report. The inferno seemed to have come to Sardinia, and everyone was thinking and talking about the fires and the losses.

Fires were not new to Sardinia, which has a history of them. Hot and dry years came in cycles, and years of fires tended to do the same. However, aridity is a condition, not the cause of fires: Were the forest fires caused by "nature" or "culture"? Most Sardinians believed that the fires were not accidents or chance events, but rather were set by people and thus were acts of human intention. The important question for Sardinians was who set them and why.

The traditional agent of fire, according to Sardinian belief, was the shepherd, who was adept at setting blazes for a variety of purposes. One well-established use of fire as part of the pastoral regime was to clear the dead plants, weeds, and bushes, unconsumable by flocks, to allow new, edible sprouts to grow from the ash-enriched soil. Here fire was used to intervene in the plant cycle. A second use of fire as part of the pastoral regime was to expand the pasture area by burning forest and clearing the way for new pasture. Loss of forest and its resources was usually resisted by communities, but we must remind ourselves that all of the Mediterranean landscape was once covered by oak forests, and the fields and pastures that dominate the landscape in modern times were brought into being by clearing the forests. A third use of fire was in the pursuit of vendettas, where arson could be directed against the pasture, livestock, buildings, property, and even persons of the opponents. A fourth object of arson was resistance against state encroachment, control, and repression, the fire being directed, much like bombs and firearms, against the property, housing, and persons of agents of the state.

Another slightly variant use of arson was against encroachment by other forces, such as commercial development. An example was the luxury tourist resorts on the northeast coast of Sardinia, the Costa Smerelda, Emerald Coast. The resorts, built by the Aga Khan, staffed and supplied more from the mainland than from Sardinia itself, were playgrounds for the Italian and international yachting class. The beautiful resorts of the Costa Smerelda have more than once in the 1980s and 1990s felt the angry tongues of flame, more often than not appearing as large brush fires. No one thought that they were acts of nature. The Sardinians of the northeast were known to be angry about these resorts which, they felt, had taken so much of the splendid Sardinian coast, and were giving so little back in the way of jobs, orders for Sardinian products, and respect for Sardinian culture. Displeasure was repeatedly expressed in fire.

However, in 1994, for once no one was pointing a finger at shepherds or at resistance to state or commercial encroachment. More "modern" motives were being attributed to the fire-starting culprits. There were two theories, one pointing to outside, foreign arsonists as sources of the fires, the other pointing to internal, local arsonists. Some Villagrandesi theorized that Germans and other foreigners had seen the beauties of Sardinia, such as its splendid forests, and become so jealous, so *invidiosi*, envious, that they felt compelled to destroy Sardinia's natural beauty. This version of the theory projects the Sardinian model of invidia onto foreigners, who may or may not be so oriented. Given the abundant beauty of central and northern European forests, those espousing this theory did not make an informed assessment of the likelihood that northern Europeans would be envious of Sardinian forests.

The other somewhat more sophisticated version of this theory, presented to me by more highly educated Villagrandesi, was that the fires were set by professional agents of external, non-Sardinian tourist areas that competed with Sardinia for tourist dollars, lire, or marks. This conspiracy theory, once again a highland model, but this time of competitive behavior projected onto outsiders, might have been more credible if the fires had been in the coastal areas, where at least 90 percent of the tourists spend all of their time, rather than in the interior, where tourist traffic and dollars are more a gleam in the eye of local residents than an established reality. For most tourists, Sardinia is sea, sun, and sand, with only a few of the adventurous and hardy venturing into the mountains, such as the occasional German bicyclists peddling determinedly up the steep mountain roads. This amazes the locals, who rarely bike, but when they do, ride their bikes down the mountains and then truck them back up. (The image of Sardinia as sea, sun, and sand is difficult to overcome even by the anthropologist who has spent two, agonizing, freezing winters in an unheated and humid stone house in the mountains.) Most Sardinians did not favor these theories that blamed foreign arsonists, preferring to blame their own compatriots.

By far, the most popular and discussed theory was that local Sardinians were setting the fires to get jobs. Two of the largest job schemes in inland and highland Sardinia were rimboscamento and anti-incendi. Those without jobs in reforestation or fire-fighting wanted them, and those with part-time or occasional jobs wanted full-time or permanent jobs. As mentioned previously, these were very good jobs with guaranteed security and full government benefits and were regarded as prizes by the local population. The logic went: One way to increase the number of jobs available in reforestation and fire-fighting would be to have more fires and more destroyed forests; job-seekers were simply advancing their own causes by starting fires. This theory might seem unduly paranoid, if some occasional employees of the reforestation scheme in southern Ogliastra had not been caught, red-handed, setting a fire (*La Nuova*, 14 August 1994:3). (You may also remember the case a few years ago of two young fire fighters in California arrested for starting what became a huge and destructive fire.) The Sardinian newspapers (e.g., *L'Unione Sarda*, 13 August 1994:1) began to call the fires "green terrorism" aimed at increasing the funds directed to environmental projects and thus the jobs available under those projects. Once again, we see that in highland Sardinia the struggle to gain a permanent, secure job, a posto fisso, was a serious obsession.

We can, however, look beyond the immediate strivings and delicts of individuals to more general causes of the devastating fires of 1994. The burning of the forests, pastures, fields, and even orchards and vineyards was possible because of the depopulation of the countryside—the absence of highland townspeople who once occupied much of the terrain on a regular basis as they pursued their multi-faceted livestock-rearing pastoralism, and garden, field, and orchard cultivation. The local population had in the past supervised the countryside and cooperated and worked together to block and stop fires. As *L'Unione Sarda* (13 August 94:1) put it,

> Those who live in the rural towns understand what has happened:
> once all of the people, armed with torches [for counter fires] and a
> spirit of survival, agreed to defend nature from fire. But they had a
> primary interest: to save the fields of grain, the flocks, the vines,
> the forests where cattle and pigs found nourishment, the pastures
> where they raised the sheep and goats. . . . [Now] there are ever
> fewer people working the land. [my translation]

It was not only the absence of people, but the absence of livestock that made the countryside more vulnerable to fire. The undergrowth and dead plants that once would have been cleared by sheep, goats, cattle, and horses, remained on the ground, ready to be tinder for fire (*La Nuova*, 14 August 1994:3).

What were the causes of this depopulation of the countryside? One was the unattractiveness of rural work to young people brought up with the urban values taught by national schooling and the mass media, especially television (Salzman 1996b) and magazines. Young Sardinian highlanders say, "We don't want to be peasants." Their grandparents were aghast at this glib dismissal of rural work, and said that it is a sin to leave the terraces, the fields and pastures, and the orchards and vineyards unused and deteriorating. And it was true that the main productive resources available in the region were agricultural and pastoral resources. A second reason for the depopulation of the countryside was the belief that agriculture and pastoralism were very hard work, were insecure, and did not pay well, in comparison with posti fissi, secure, permanent jobs. This may be true, if somewhat exaggerated, but might have been, or should have been, outweighed by the fact that there were very few permanent, salaried jobs available. Third, various kinds of agricultural subsidies, often from the EEC, for not planting certain crops or not producing milk or livestock, had encouraged people to look to bureaucratic payments rather than rural production. It certainly did not get people on the land when they were paid to stay off of it. Fourth, various external agencies, such as the Forest Rangers and the fire-fighters, had been given responsibility for taking care of the countryside, thus undermining the responsibility of local people for protecting their own natural and constructed resources. Fifth, many laws and regulations, perhaps reasonable in the abstract for their particular purposes, had been put into place, and these unfortunately impeded other important processes, such as control of fires. For example, roads could not be made in forests without state permission; anti-fire protectors could not be attached to cork oaks; counter-fires to stop fires were forbidden; flocks, which would have cleared forest floors of inflammable vegetable matter, were not allowed into the forests; and all of these regulatory measures were increasingly and stringently enforced by the Corpo Forestale. As a result of all of these factors, "The proprietors of the land [both common and private], whether cultivators or pastoralists, have progressively lost the will to safeguard their own goods. The spirit of conservation of capital has been anaesthetized . . ." (*L'Unione Sarda*, 20 August 1994:6).

The burning of the countryside relit the controversy, always smouldering, between local inhabitants and government agencies as to who should control "local resources," as the townspeople saw it, or "natural resources," as the government saw it. Throughout central and highland Sardinia, local people were objecting to the way the fires and the environment more generally were being handled by government agencies. In Montiferri, Oristano Province, a protest meeting reported in *L'Unione Sarda* (20 August 1994:21) brought out common objections. One young woman yelled:

> The truth is that in order to save ten trees, [you implemented various measures, and in consequence] you made it possible for 10,000 trees to burn.

At that same meeting, Mario Farina, the president of the shepherds' cooperative, said:

> Enough with the rules dropped down from above. We want to manage our own territory ourselves, as our fathers have taught us. The Forest Rangers must limit themselves to guarding.

Bruno Cambula, a university student, argued:

> The Forest Rangers were not capable of coordinating the fire fighting on the ground. They did not know how to do anything but block the roads, thus keeping the shepherds from protecting their haylofts and animals.

Francesco Pes, land surveyor, pointed out:

> At a certain point [in the fire], it became clear to us that the fire could have been stopped with a counterfire. But the Forest Rangers threatened us with arrest on the spot.

Agostinangelo Cocco, shepherd of twenty-nine years, spoke the view of shepherds in Villagrande and of most shepherds throughout the land:

> Many people have had their [agricultural and pastoral] enterprises destroyed because the Forest Rangers have [in order to protect "nature"] forbidden the cleaning and plowing of the terrain. The only areas that were saved from the fire were those plowed secretly, risking fines of a half million lire. This was a disastrous policy. By now the forests are abandoned. Before they were not. As my grandfather said, the forests grew with the flocks inside. If the flocks are not there the forests are abandoned. [Banning the flocks] benefits only the fire-fighters' industry.

The fires of 1994 thus once again convinced some central and highland Sardinians that their destinies were not well protected in the hands of government agencies, and that the costs of disengagement with the countryside might involve losing it altogether. Other Sardinians saw once again the difficulties and dangers of agricultural and pastoral production, and this reaffirmed their desire for secure jobs in other sectors. But in the light of the fires, some of the prominent sources of jobs, such as forest rangering, reforestation, and fire-fighting, appeared to be themselves incompetent or corrupt, as much a part of the problem as an avoidance of it.

KIDNAPPINGS, 1995

In December 1994, prominent entrepreneur Giuseppe Vinci was kidnapped by unknown bandits. So the year 1995 began with the ongoing burden of the Vinci kidnapping and the unknown fate of the prisoner. Young Vinci and his family owned an important industry with many employees, in Macomer, the second city of Nuoro Province, home of the Romano cheese factory which exports sheep's milk cheese around the world. The presumption was that the kidnapping was motivated by money and for that reason directed at a wealthy family. (Kidnapping for ransom has been complicated by Italian law forbidding the payment of ransom and, since 1991, freezing assets belonging to the victim's family. But sometimes special permission allowing payment is given, and sometimes relatives and friends of the victim find a way to pay the ransom illegally.)

By May 1995, Vinci had been in hidden captivity for six months, and little progress toward freeing him was evident. After some initial demonstrations by the family firm's employees against the kidnapping, public response had died out. Inquiries and searches by the police and forces of state order had no result so far. Sharon Vinci, the young wife of Guiseppe, was particularly disturbed by what seemed to be the public apathy and even acceptance of the kidnapping of her husband.

There was also a second recent, ongoing, and equally unresolved kidnapping, that of Giuseppe Sircana of Calangianus, a contractor for the extraction of cork from the indigenous cork oaks of Sardinia. No apparent progress was being made in this case either.

There had always been, in highland Sardinia, a tacit acceptance if not approval of acts of banditry. In some people's view, bandits and fugitives from state justice, *latitanti*, showed the respected highland virtue *balentia*, consisting of courage, daring, and shrewdness, and they stood for local norms above those of the external and foreign state. These *banditi* and fugitives, according to this view, were "our own," of the highland towns, and deserved support and protection. Furthermore, to some extent members of other towns were fair game for livestock rustling, robbery, or kidnapping, and this was especially so of rich families, who could be assumed to have stolen from the others, and foreigners from outside of the highlands, who had no claim on solidarity or protection.

Even among those highlanders who did not sanction banditry, many held to the highland norm that each family minded its own business and did not interfere in the business of others. The highland rule was that offenses or attacks were the business of those directly involved and would have to be dealt with by those parties alone. So for many highlanders, self-help in righting wrongs done to you and your family and neutrality in regard to other people's quarrels, were more than just a personal strategy, they were a way of life with community moral sanction.

The highland norms of self-help and neutrality, of vendetta and local solidarity, have come gradually, especially in the post-World War II period, to be increasingly seen as outmoded, inappropriate, and immoral. With increasing education, mass media, and travel since World War I and especially World War II, strictly local, town loyalties have been challenged by the broader solidarities of highlanders, Sardinians, Italians, Catholics, and human beings. Practical constraints of communication, transportation, and firepower have also changed, with state authorities being more effective in demanding the monopoly of coercive force and more efficient in imposing order.

Perhaps more important was the appreciation of many highlanders that their future opportunities rested not in closed, rural communities but in a modernizing, developing region open to the world. Many highlanders, who wanted modern jobs from an expansion of tourism, the establishment of new factories, and new economic investment generally, viewed vendettas, banditry, and kidnapping as negative inhibitions to the desirable development of Sardinia and to employment opportunities for themselves and their children. Commentators, such as reporters, columnists, letter-writers in Sardinian newspapers (Cao 1995; Floris 1995), three labour union leaders (Nieddu, Uda, and Mereu 1995), the president of the Region of Sardinia, F. Palomba, in a letter to the president of the council (i.e. Prime Minister Dini of Italy) (*L'Unione Sarda*, 19 May 1995:3), and even the captives pleading with their kidnappers (Fiori 1978, in De Gionannis and Serri 1991) argued that kidnappings and other banditry would chase away entrepreneurs and scare away investment, thus undermining the desired development and improved opportunities for highlanders and leaving Sardinia underdeveloped. Thus we can see that some highlanders held to the old ways, some to the hoped-for new way, and many others were torn by conflicting norms and dreams.

So the battle, for Sharon Vinci, was not just with the kidnappers, but with the public as well. Could the public be mobilized to give overt and emphatic support to the kidnapped and to withhold support and approval from the kidnappers? Those hoping for mobilization against kidnapping and banditry argued that silence was equivalent to complicity with the kidnappers (*L'Unione Sarda*, 10 May 1995:1). Three activities were organized for demonstrating public support: signing petitions demanding the return of Vinci; hanging white sheets from windows and balconies to show solidarity with Vinci and opposition to the kidnappers; torchlight processions with banners and signs demanding freedom for Vinci. In Macomer, 12,000 names supported the petition, and participation in the processions and the hanging of sheets was strong. In Nuoro, the provincial capital, the hanging of sheets was spotty, but some women showed their support by hanging out their best, hand-decorated sheets from their dowries. In Nuoro the torchlight procession was 5,000 strong.

The kidnappings and their consequences were not solely local matters of face-to-face relations. Radio Barbagia devoted twelve straight hours to the kidnappings on 15 May 1995, with calls not only from the families and friends of the kidnapped and from public figures, but from individuals and families involved in previous kidnappings (*L'Unione Sarda*, 16 May 1995:3). The Vinci kidnapping was also made a feature story on the Italian television program *Tempo Reale*, which had sent reporters and cameramen to the Nuoro demonstrations (*L'Unione Sarda*, 16 May 1995:14; 17 May 1995:12), and thus became national Italian news.

In spite of the campaign for solidarity with the kidnapped, not everyone was won over. In Orgosolo, the highland town renown and notorious for its banditi and its resistance to the state, graffiti appeared on the church which said "Vinci, we want money," i.e., Vinci family, if you want Giuseppe freed, pay us the ransom; "Vinci pay more," and "Sharon, pay or Vinci dies" (*L'Unione Sarda*, 15 May 1995:1)—sentiments, obviously, siding with the kidnappers. And, from apathy or in support of the kidnappers, no sheets were hung out in solidarity with the kidnapped. The reporter equated this silence with "a culture of non-intervention" (Selloni, *L'Unione Sarda*, 16 May 1995:3).

Just as all of these events were taking place in highland Barbagia, in the Province of Nuoro, kidnappers struck again, on Mothers' Day, 14 May 1995, in Abbasanta, in the western, lowland province of Oristano, carrying off a sixty-seven-year-old woman, farm owner Vanna Licheri Leone. Yet another shock, another blow. The authorities, following the law, froze all of the assets of the Leone family, in order to make it impossible to pay the ransom. (The Italian law banning ransom payments and requiring the freezing of familial assets was controversial at that time and has continued to be so in relation to more recent kidnappings [*Corriere della Sera*, 28 January 1998:4–5].) This third kidnapping, of Vanna Leone, elicited bitter commentary. Liori (1995:1), also author of *The Manual for Survival in Barbagia*, wrote,

> Our beloved land has chosen to live by theft—of whatever type, be it kidnapping or unjustified government subsidies, highway robbery or pensions unjustified by need—and have chucked out the window the pride of production. [The valued highland virtue] *balentía* does not anymore mean taking responsibility on oneself

and defending to the limit one's property: the definition is now that of enriching oneself easily at the expense of others, whether private individuals or the state.

Lead newspaper stories asserted that "there grows in all of our Island anger against the anonymous kidnappers" (*L'Unione Sarda*, 16 May 1995:1).

Reinforcements arrived to bolster the state forces of order. By the 17th of May, fifty additional police were sent to join the Crime Prevention Nucleus of Sardinia, and thirty-five Carabinieri national police arrived from Calabria on the mainland to join the Carbinieri unit, Hunters of Sardinia. These groups were sent to establish roadblocks and examine vehicles and to scour the vast, largely unpopulated countryside of the high plateau, a rugged landscape of mountains, valleys, and Mediterranean oak forests. This central, highland region, full of caves, sheltered crevices, and hidden pockets, was known well only by the highland shepherds who grazed their sheep on the high plateau.

It is taken for granted in Sardinia that the world of the shepherd shaded into the world of the *latitante*, fugitive, and the bandito. This shading from one world to another was felt to be both geographical and cultural, both physical and behavioral. It was in the same remote high plateau and mountains where the shepherds took their flocks that the fugitives from state law were believed to hide, to which the bandits retreated, and where kidnappers sequestered their prisoners. The shepherds' traditional rustling of sheep and the graded combat among noi pastori, sometimes up to blood vendetta, seemed a small step from the rustling, or kidnapping, of people, to be fleeced of money rather than wool, and from the robbery and attacks against those outside of the shepherd milieu. The shepherds' penchant for firearms, justified as necessary for defense of the flocks, could be seen as hard to distinguish from that of outlaws.

While the modest numbers of newly reenforced agents of order were requested and applauded by local Sardinian officials, such as mayors, commentators were quick to warn against any heavy-handed intervention by the authorities, as in a wholesale invasion by the army, which had happened in the past, lest there be a backlash of public opinion. This point was put indirectly but clearly by Pititu ("Ma è sbagliato reagire a testa bassa," *L'Unione Sarda*, 16 May 1995:3).

> In this dramatic moment it would not be useful to have dramatic actions, visits by the highest authorities, or extraordinary interventions. As in each combat that one is losing, reacting by bowing one's head, by accepting the humiliation, is no way to recuperate. Rather, it is necessary to put the appropriate countermeasures in place, those that would be that much more efficient for having been considered carefully, to deal with this extreme emergency. No one

must be persuaded to strike unwise, impulsive, and inopportune attitudes that would risk serving only the interests of the kidnappers.

Even with the growing anger against the kidnapping, actions by state authorities, which seem to be attacks on Sardinia and Sardinians in general, risked eliciting a defensive reaction that rejected the state and was more willing to support or at least tolerate other Sardinians, whatever acts they might be involved in. So the authorities, local Sardinian as well as mainland Italian, were faced with a bit of a balancing act: they had to act swiftly and decisively in pursuing the kidnappers, but without disturbing or overwhelming and thus offending and insulting the Sardinian populace.

Then on the 18th of May—"It's war; it's an open challenge to the State" (*L'Unione Sarda*, 19 May 1995:1)—another businessman, Ferruccio Checchi, proprietor of a hotel at the beach resort of Cala Gonone, Dorgali, was kidnapped. This was the day that, at Nuoro, the provincial capital, there were celebrations for the festa of the police. And at Cala Gonone, the kidnapping itself took place just after the Checchi family had watched on national television the program, *Tempo Reale*, about the kidnappings of Vinci and the others. Even worse, the kidnappers originally had intended to carry off the three-year-old daughter of the Checchi family, together with her Somali nanny, and failed only because the child was asleep in another part of the house, so they took the father instead. In response, a summit of the forces of order was called, and one hundred elite army parachutists were brought to Barbagia. The hotelkeepers of Cala Gonone called the kidnapping "A mortal blow to tourism and our economy," and President Scalfaro of the Italian Republic lamented "a wound to the heart of a generous land" (*L'Unione Sarda*, 20 May 1995:1).

In towns and cities throughout Sardinia, demonstrations were called in opposition to the kidnappings. Although Villagrande and Ogliastra had not been touched directly by the kidnappings of 1995, a torchlight parade was called in Villagrande for 25 May, to be followed by a discussion. The parade was well attended, perhaps partly because the scope was conceived broadly as "solidarity in confronting kidnappings and against criminality," to attract those who had more immediate concerns about murder, bombings, theft, vandalism, drugs, etc.

Kidnapping itself was far from unknown in Ogliastra and Villagrande. One of those to march in Nuoro was Berardi, the head of the industrialists of Nuoro Province, whose daughter, Cristina, had been kidnapped in 1987 (during the time of my first visit to Sardinia) and held for 120 days before being discovered on a forested hillside near the Villagrande border and liberated by a police search party (*La Nuova Sardegna*, 20 October 1987, in De Gioannis and Serri 1991:151–52). Two decades previous, in 1967, Peppino Catte, who had a trout farm at an artificial lake in Villagrande territory, was kidnapped nearby and held for twenty days, until the bandits were convinced that he was not rich enough to pay ransom and released him (Fiori 1978, in De Gioannis and Serri 1991:147–50). In both of these cases, the guards and the prisoner moved considerable distances by foot almost every night, from one hiding spot to another, remaining in hiding during the day. Catte estimated that in twenty nights he had walked four hundred kilometers overland, in the dark. He lost sixteen kilos. Cristina Berardi had to be carried across the roughest and steepest terrain by her captors. But in the end, both Cristina Berardi and Peppino Catte were fortunate, for over the years many of those kidnapped in Sardinia never returned home.

Nor has Ogliastra been without its bandits and fugitives from the law, some of whom were in 1995 the most famous and feared in all of Sardinia. Pasquale Stocchino, a fugitive from 1972, when five persons were killed in a failed kidnapping, was still at liberty in 1995. Stocchino was from Arzana, the town to the south of Villagrande, sometimes called the Orgosolo of the south. Adolfo Cavia, a fugitive since 1983, when he was involved with a kidnapping, was still at large in 1995. Cavia came from Urzulei, the second town to the north of Villagrande (*L'Unione Sarda*, 20 May 1995:4; *Panorama*, 2 June 1995:38–39). People thought of these fugitives first whenever important crimes were committed, especially crimes similar to those in which they were known to have been involved previously. Beyond the established fugitives, four shepherds, Mario and Costantino Cabiddu, Gianluigi Olians, and Pierluigi Melis, residents of Villanova, the *frazione* of Villagrande up on the high plateau, along with the shepherd Alberto Stochino of Arzana, were indicted in 1992 for a role in the 1984 kidnapping of a young, engaged couple, Franco Pisano and Annalisa Pittau, from Mandas in Cagliari Province (*L'Unione Sarda*, 6 July 1991:19). So the problem of kidnapping was by no means foreign to Ogliastrini and Villagrandesi in particular.

During this same period of kidnapping and public response, in May 1995, a loud echo of an earlier kidnapping was heard. Farouk Kassam, a young boy who had been abducted in 1992 from his family's residence in the Costa Smeralda, was, in May 1995, along with his family, quitting Sardinia and returning to France, the natal home of his mother, Marion Bleriot, in order to go to French school, as the move was explained by the parents. The kidnapping of Farouk was something of an anomaly, for in general the objects of Sardinian kidnappings had been adults rather than children (notwithstanding the recent, failed attempt to kidnap the Checchi child). The Costa Smeralda, where Farouk's father owned a restaurant, must have appeared an attractive target. Farouk's parents could be expected to pay a good ransom for their son.

The kidnappers of Farouk could not have imagined the reaction. The Kassam family was by no means amenable to playing by the kidnappers' rules and was very vocal in rejecting not only the kidnapping of their son but the validity of the kidnapping. Marion Bleriot especially was eloquent, and her appeals to the mothers of Sardinia touched a nerve that had never quite been touched before. The mothers of Barbagia were asked to speak out against violence, and they did take that unusual step, as was reported in newspaper accounts: "Voices of women for Farouk" (*L'Unione Sarda*, 23 January 1992:25) and "Women in Barbagia: . . . the female role in regard to kidnappings" (*L'Unione Sarda*, 28 January 1992). Bleriot went so far as to go to Orgosolo, the symbolic heart of Barbagia, and speak from the pulpit of the church to the mothers of Orgosolo. It was for Farouk that sheets were for the first time hung from windows and balconies in solidarity. And it was for Farouk that public opinion shifted in Barbagia, to a greater rejection than ever of kidnapping and banditry. In the end, the foreignness of the Kassam family probably worked against the kidnappers, for the family came to be seen, at least by many Sardinians, as guests of Sardinia, and their treatment as a reflection on Sardinia. After an intensive search, and perhaps with the assistance of a famous or infamous jailed ex-fugitive, the forces of order finally liberated Farouk. Public opinion had not changed radically, but it had shifted significantly against kidnapping and banditry. For this reason, Sharon Vinci was not starting from scratch.

The four kidnappings of 1995 ended diversely (*Corriere della Sera*, 28 January 1998; personal communication from M.L.M. of Villagrande, 10 May 1998):

> **Giuseppe Vinci**, fifteen kilos lighter in weight, returned to his family after 310 days of captivity, set free by his kidnappers in the vicinity of Talana, the town to the north of Villagrande, after a ransom payment of three and a half billion lire, over two million U.S. dollars. [Whether this payment was authorized by special permission or was paid illegally, I do not know. In the 1997 kidnapping of Silvia Melis, ransom was paid without state permission, and the businessman who paid US$800,000 has been indicted and will be tried (*Corriere della Sera*, 28 January 1998:5).] For the kidnapping of Giuseppe Vinci, five shepherds from Orgosolo and other highland towns have been arrested and are being tried.

> **Ferrucio Checchi**, after five months and three days in captivity, was liberated in the vicinity of Oliena by the Carabinieri. No ransom had been paid. Four men, including three shepherds from Orgosolo, Loculi, and Oliena were arrested and are being tried.

> **Giuseppe Sircana** has never been seen again. A shepherd from Loculi has been arrested.

Vanna Licheri has never been seen again. No arrests have been made.

The summer of 1995 was unusual for kidnappings in Sardinia, for it was rare that as many as four prisoners were held by kidnappers at any one time. In the years 1980–1988, there were all together thirty-seven known kidnappings in Sardinia, an annual average of 4.1, with individual years ranging from two kidnappings in three different years to eight in 1984 (De Gioannis and Serri 1991:158, table 3). During the same years, there was an annual average of 94.5 robberies, 35.5 murders, and 436.2 cases of livestock rustling (De Gioannis and Serra 1991:158, table 3). To these statistics might be added those of the population of Sardinian shepherds who migrated, with their flocks, to the Italian mainland, especially to Tuscany and surrounding regions, mainly during the 1960s (Solinas 1989). At the turn of the year in 1990–91, I was visiting friends in Tuscany, and saw on the national news the liberation of a Tuscan prisoner and the arrest of his kidnappers, and found myself saying to myself, "Oh, let the kidnappers not be Sardinian shepherds," but they were.

My account might make Sardinia seem a very dangerous place. Certainly at the end of the nineteenth century, Sardinia led, by magnitudes of up to twenty times or 2000 percent, all Italian regions in murders, usurpation and damage to property, arson, and theft, in relation to population (De Gioannis and Serri 1991:156, table 1). But by 1982, the rate of criminality in relation to population generally was much lower in Sardinia than in Italy, 662.4 crimes of all types for 100,000 inhabitants in Sardinia, compared to 1,135.3 per 100,000 in Italy overall. In Sardinia crimes against the person were 125.9, in comparison to 261.9 in Italy overall (De Gioannis and Serri 1991:157, table 2; cp. ISTAT 1991:85, table 6.4, for 1989 figures). However, within Sardinia, the rates of rustling, kidnapping, and murder were highest in Nuoro Province, the central, highland zone, which during the period 1980–88 accounted for 60 percent of the kidnappings, half of the rustling, and almost half of the homicides in Sardinia (De Gioannis and Serri 1991:158, table 3), in spite of being the least populated of Sardinia's four provinces.

CONCLUSION

The lives of highland Sardinians were shaped by both their cultural presumptions and their positions in their society and in the wider world. Culture and position provided, as we might describe it, the tools and resources upon which people could draw as they dealt with life, and also the burdens that they had to carry and the constraints within which they had to work. The tools and the burdens, the resources and the constraints, were manifested in people's engagements in the different events that marked different moments of the calendar and of their lives. It was in these events that culture and position ceased being abstractions and potentialities and came alive as influences in the actions of individuals and the movements of collectivities. It was in response to the challenges and opportunities posed by events of various types that the significance of culture and position were played out, and it was in the playing out that culture and position could be changed.

Chapter Four

Comparing Events

Examining people's lives in particular societies—such as the Yarahmadzai of Baluchistan or Villagrande in highland Ogliastra—through an exploration of various events is the ethnographic task of anthropology. The study of events provides insight into how a particular social setting and the cultural ideas that are present shape people's lives and how people, pursuing their lives, reinforce or reform social arrangements and cultural frameworks.

In this ethnographic task, the anthropologist approaches an understanding of people's lives by two mutually supportive strategies. One approach is to *observe people in action*, engaged in the events that occupy their minds and activities, as has been recounted in my accounts of the Sarhad of Baluchistan and highland Sardinia. The other approach is to take a step back in order to gain greater perspective, by placing people's goals, concerns, and worries, as manifested in the events in which they participate, within a wider *context* of historical developments, social processes and cultural concepts.

This *contextualization*, which has been included in our previous discussions of events in Baluchistan and Sardinia, provides insights into the more general, underlying influences both generated by people's activities and affecting people's lives. For example, to take a case of historical contextualization, encapsulation of the Baluch by the government of Iran forced the Yarahmadzai to abandon raiding and provided an opportunity for them to take up trading. Another example of contextualization involves the Italian national institutions, such as schools and television, which disparaged rural labor. Thus, people in rural Sardinia who were exposed to the values espoused by these external influences preferred to abandon cultivation and pastoralism and to seek urban-type, white-collar jobs.

Ethnographic description and contextualization provide an obligatory basis for understanding human life and human lives. But the anthropological task is not finished when ethnographic accounts of particular cultures are completed. Two important steps to more complete knowledge remain. One step is to assess the validity of our ethnographic interpretations. How do we know that our ethnographic contextualizations are correct? Is there some way to check our understandings? The other step is to try to construct more general understandings of the ways in which events interplay with human lives. How can we raise our understanding above the particular ethnographic cases we have examined, so that our formulations are relevant to people elsewhere? Are our understandings of pastoral nomads in Baluchistan applicable to pastoral nomads in Africa? Do schools and television discourage people from engaging in rural production in China as well as in Italy? Is there some way to gain general knowledge that is widely applicable?

Anthropologists do have a tool to aid them in trying to establish the validity of their interpretations and to formulate more general understandings. This tool is *comparison*, juxtaposing different cases to see if the contextualizations of different individual cases are logically consistent and if insights about one case apply to others (Nadel 1952; Eggan 1954; Nader 1994). For example, I have argued, about highland Sardinian communities, that acts of invidia, envy, are strongly present mainly in egalitarian communities and only found between people who perceive themselves to be peers. If we compare events in Sardinian communities resulting from envy, as I have interpreted them, with other ethnographic cases of other people in other places, such as Spain, Africa, and Japan, and we find that this argument seems to fit among them as well, then we can feel more confident about our understanding of Sardinian communities. And we can also begin to feel that we have grasped a more general principle of social life—that events arising from envy are found mainly between equals, or, even more generally, that people tend to compare their own situations only with people whom they consider to be their equals, and do not compare their situations with people they consider to be their superiors or inferiors.

We can also compare events among the same people during different times, different historical periods. For example, we can compare pre-1928, pre-encapsulation Baluchistan with post-1935, encapsulated Baluchistan, after the Baluch were pacified. To take an obvious example, we could compare events involving Yarahmadzai tribesmen temporarily leaving Baluchistan in order to exploit external resources and bring income back to the Sarhad. In the pre-encapsulation period, these events were predatory raiding against Persian villages and caravans. In the post-encapsulation period, these events were mainly laboring for pay or bringing trade goods across borders and forwarding them to Persian cities. The difference between the two periods was the free use of violent coercion against outsiders by the Baluchi tribesmen during the first period, and during the second the effective suppression of Baluchi violence against Persians by the militarily more powerful Iranian government. This comparison allows us to formulate the more general understanding, which we can call "the gun rule": he who holds the gun, makes the rules. In other words, the state apparatus always claims the monopoly of coercion, and when the state effectively controls a region, local people have to find ways other than violence to achieve their goals.

Comparing events allows us to step back beyond contextualization, to gain an even broader perspective. We take off our ethnographer's hat, and, replacing it with our comparative anthropologist's hat, seek more general understandings. At this stage, we try to go beyond our accounts of Baluchistan and Sardinia and other particular places and times, to gain insights about humankind more generally, and the circumstances under which different kinds of events arise. This is the immodest goal of this modest chapter, which must be little more than an illustration and an attempt to step in the right direction. Let us try to build on our already established understandings of Baluchistan and Sardinia by using these two cases for our comparing of events.

MIGRATING

Migrating is always a noteworthy event in both Baluchistan and Sardinia. The well-being of the flocks, and of the people who depend upon the livestock in making a living, depends upon it. In both places, one of the main aims of migration is to provide the sheep and goats with the best available grazing, water, and temperature, in an environment safe from disease and from predators, both animal and human. The objective of the spatial movement is, ironically, maintaining constant conditions; the goal of migration is constancy of moderate temperatures, adequate humidity, and availability of pasturage for the flock. People move to assure unvarying, favorable conditions for their animals.

While pastoral migration is very important in both Baluchistan and Sardinia, the nature of migration in the two places is different in important respects. Let us begin by considering timing and destination. One way of describing an important difference is by saying that migration in Baluchistan is more an adaptation to unpredictable micro-environmental variations, differences in short distances and periods, while movement of the flocks in Sardinia is more an adaptation to predictable macro-environmental variations, differences in long distances and periods.

In Sardinia, the migration pattern is what is referred to in Europe, where the pattern is common, as "transhumance." This migration responds to two macro-environmental variations: (1) differences in altitude with attendant variations in climate; and (2) seasonal variations with attendant differences in climate. In transhumance, climate is "controlled" by changing altitudes as the seasons change. Specifically, the cold temperatures and snow of winter in the highlands are avoided by moving the flocks to the mild temperatures of lowland valleys or plains, and the hot temperatures and dried up vegetation of summer in lowland plains and valleys are avoided by moving the flocks to the mountain highlands where temperatures are cooler and the grass watered by melted winter snow is fresh.

The timing of migration in transhumance is regular and predictable, for it follows the seasons. There are only two main moves; to the highlands for the summer, and to the lowlands for the winter. These predictable destinations make possible permanent bases. Sardinian shepherds have built ovili, consisting usually of a rude hut for the shepherd and a corral for the animals, in the highlands, and often in the lowlands also. They thus are migrating between two permanent bases, their sheep stations. In recent times, with the aid of money from what is now called the European Union, some have added solar panels for electricity to run electric lights and refrigerators or televisions.

In contrast, in the Sarhad of Baluchistan, where the sheep and goats stay on the high plateau the year-round, migration is primarily a response to micro-environmental variations. Rainfall is highly erratic and unpredictable in the Sarhad, and in consequence so is vegetation that the flocks can consume as pasturage. So it is not known beforehand where in the tribal territory rain will fall and grass will grow. People have to wait, keep a keen eye, collect information from all who are travelling around, and then see where there is good pasturage, where it is not too crowded with other herding camps and flocks, where there is good water available, where there is disease to be avoided, where enemy groups might be, and then decide when and where they will move. So the Baluch never know much ahead of time exactly when they will migrate or what their destination will be, other than staying within their large, tribal territory. This is why the migration pattern of any herding camp differs from one year to the next, and why the migration pattern of each herding camp will differ from that of every other.

Another important difference in the kind of migration found in Baluchistan and Sardinia is the nature of the social unit migrating. In Sardinia, the shepherd migrates with his herding partner or partners, if he has any, and his assistants, either sons or hired hands. Other family and household members, including females of all ages, and sons too young or incapable of engaging in pastoralism, the infirm aged, and any other dependent males, live separately and apart from the sheep stations, in the town where the permanent, family house functions as a home base. In other words, families as wholes, and the larger community, are not nomadic. They are sedentary, living permanently in stable dwellings, stone houses, in the town. In contrast, among the nomadic tribes of the Sarhad of Baluchistan, migration is always undertaken by full households, including all members irrespective of sex, age, and capacity; no one is left behind in this fully nomadic society. The entire community, in the form of the herding camp, is nomadic, migrating repeatedly during the annual cycle of productive activities. Furthermore, while in Sardinia each family flock is taken on the transhumance independently by its shepherds, among the Sarhadi tribes the set of households forming the herding camp migrate together, collectively.

These differences between migration in Sardinia and Baluchistan—(1) the regularity of seasonal and altitudinal transhumance vs. the irregularity of opportunistic nomadic movement; (2) the individuality of Sardinian transhumance vs. the collective migration of Baluchi herding camps; and (3) the split of the household in Sardinia between the town residence and the countryside sheep stations vs. the unified households in the nomadic community groups of Baluchistan—reflected important differences in the lives of Sardinians and Baluch. One difference was that the regular transhumance in Sardinia was relatively simple, while in Baluchistan the multiple annual migrations, always involving arduous shifts in household residences and property, was complicated, involving extensive collection of information about environmental conditions, as well as intensive consultations and negotiations among the divergent factions that made up the herding camp. In Sardinia, transhumance was largely a technical measure involving flocks; in Baluchistan, it was a political decision of communities.

A second consequence was the social and cultural divergence, in Sardinia, between the shepherds in the pastures and the women in the town. The individuality, competition, and danger of the pastures and of the lives of the men, contrasted with the sociability and security in the towns and in the lives of the women. The shepherds and the women of their families led somewhat differentiated, independent lives, separated spatially as they were much of the time, and entrusted with different but equally important family responsibilities. This degree of social and cultural divergence and independence did not exist traditionally within families among the nomadic tribesmen and tribeswomen of Baluchistan, because the family migrated together and resided together, the women and men cooperating directly in household production.

Developments since World War II intensified somewhat these differences between Sardinia and Baluchistan. Formal education outside of the household became more important in both places, as it has became more closely tied to occupational structures in the broader societies. In Sardinia, with the boys out in the sheep stations, it was the girls in the towns who had greater access to education, just as it was the senior females in households who kept the family money, records, and dealt with governmental and other external agencies. In Baluchistan, women were productive and active forces in their nomadic communities, but formal education required leaving home and going to a sedentary school, which cultural norms of modesty discouraged. As a result, in the nomadic tribes of Baluchistan, it was the boys who were sent away to school, and the girls remained limited to local knowledge. The gap in knowledge between men and women increased when Baluchi men began to leave their homes for periods of military service, migrant labor, or mobile trading, from which they gained new and marketable skills and a familiarity with the wider world. So Sardinian highland women became educated and developed modern occupational skills, while their men pursued traditional rural production; in contrast, Baluchi men began to be educated and to develop urban occupational skills, while Baluchi women remained in herding camps maintaining the nomadic home base.

COPING WITH DROUGHT

Recurrent droughts offered a repeated challenge to both highland Sardinians and Baluchi tent-dwellers. During the nineteenth century, the costs of local and regional droughts in both highland Sardinia and the Sarhad of Baluchistan were covered by predatory extraction from outsiders. The Sardinians engaged in rustling and banditry, probably at an increased rate during bad years, usually individually, but sometimes in small groups. During the period 1890–93, there were more per capita crimes against persons and property in Sardinia than in any other Italian region, including Sicily (De Gioannis and Serri 1991:156, table 1). This violent form of self-help probably led, through predation, to some redistribution of wealth from Sardinian regions and sectors which were better off, or less badly hit by drought, to communities and regions hard hit by drought. Similarly, the Sarhadi raiders usually rode beyond the borders of Baluchistan to prey on Persian caravans and peasant villages. While predatory raiding was an ongoing enterprise, it would not be surprising if raiding was intensified during periods of drought. In these respects, the response to drought in Sardinia and Baluchistan during the nineteenth century included similar strategies.

By the second half of the twentieth century, drought-related strategies in Baluchistan and Sardinia diverged somewhat. Baluchi tribesmen and tribeswomen of the Sarhad came to rely more on drought-resistant forms of rural production, especially irrigation cultivation, and on alternative, peaceable forms of foreign extraction, mainly migrant labor and mobile trading. In contrast, Sardinians came to rely more on extracting resources from the governments of the Region of Sardinia, of Italy, and of the European Union. Sardinian rural producers have become eligible for production subsidies, development aid, and disaster relief, such as drought relief payments. By the early 1990s in Europe, running a business, a household-based, rural business as much as any other kind, depended as much upon one's capability in milking government agencies and shearing aid offerings as in milking sheep and shearing wool. "School learning," most commonly on the part of shepherds' wives, sisters, and daughters, was put to good use in searching out government grant programs, analyzing their terms, manipulating the data about one's own situation, preparing forms and documents, and following up with bureaucrats to insure success in receiving payments (see also Solinas, Becucci, and Grilli 1996).

FORMING COMMUNITIES

Both Baluchi tribesmen and tribeswomen and Sardinian highlanders were born into territorial groups which were their ultimate, most inclusive, referents of political loyalty. For Sarhadi tent-dwellers, the tribe, defined by them in terms of descent from a common ancestor, was the largest political group to which they owed loyalty. The tribe collectively held the territory upon which the members lived and sought a living. Prior to conquest by the Persian state apparatus, the tribes of the Sarhad were effectively independent polities. Similarly, for Sardinian highlanders, the comune was the largest political group to which they owed political loyalty. The comune, which followed the form of the ancient Greek city-state, consisted of a nucleated town surrounded by a substantial territory, most commonly available for agriculture and pastoralism, with perhaps some smaller villages or scattered settlements as well. Residential membership gave rights of access to communal resources, such as land, water, and forests, and a presumption of mutual support and protection against external threats. The Sardinian comuni, previously under the colonial control of various countries, were eventually incorporated into the Italian state, where they formed the lowest level of territorial government, the municipality.

Within these established, territorial groups of several thousand individuals, people formed relationships to provide themselves with assistance in making a living and in assuring security. These social relationships were formed in different ways in the deserts of Baluchistan and highland Sardinia. In Baluchistan, tribesmen and tribeswomen formed collectivities, *corporate groups* with clear boundaries, to satisfy their purposes. For example, within their tribes, Sarhadi Baluch belonged by birth to a nesting set of larger and smaller corporate lineage groups, each defined by an ancestor more or less distant. They could call upon these lineage groups for assistance and support. These lineages were contingent groups, in that they became operative only when circumstances required it and individuals called them into play. At the same time, the Baluch formed limited-term, but ongoing herding camps, to provide themselves with cooperative herding groups and mobile residential communities. Thus in social relations, the Baluch leaned toward forming bounded, corporate groups with obligations of collective responsibility—"all for one, and one for all."

In Sardinia, within the comune and between comuni, highlanders, each representing his or her corporate, nuclear household and working on its behalf, operated as individuals. They struck limited and usually informal relationships, dyadic, face-to-face ties, with other individuals and, by doing so, linked into boundless and extensive but informal networks of friends spread widely over space, beyond their comune boundaries to other comuni, to cities, and even beyond Sardinia and through time. (For a general discussion of social networks in the Mediterranean, see Boissevain 1974.) For example, Sardinian shepherds in the pastures depended upon their friends and their friends' friends to collect information, such as who had rustled their sheep and whether and for how much it would be possible to ransom them.

Contracting to establish or revise a herding camp community in Baluchistan, an event that often saw a dramatic shift in camp personnel, was paralleled in Sardinia by the more informal and seemingly amorphous building of dyadic friendships and hooking up to extensive networks. In Sardinia prior to World War II, men's and women's social lives tended to be separate. Women associated with women in family homes, at the public fountains where water was collected for family needs, at the river where women washed clothes, and in the streets of the residential neighborhoods. Men associated with men, greeting and talking in the central public square, *piazza*, and in the bars, where hours were spent playing cards and talking. More than recreation and relaxation, these visits were opportunities for shepherds to collect information about livestock and cheese prices, potential herding partners, availability of pastureland, rustling, labor opportunities, government subsidies, and vendettas, among other things. Equally important, the visits were also opportunities for observing the comportment of other men, and for establishing informal "friendships," which could lead to sharing of information and limited kinds of assistance, and which were the major social resource, after the comune, available to the Sardinian shepherds.

In sum, Baluchi tribesmen and tribeswomen were enveloped, cocooned, in a nesting set of corporate lineage groups, all of which existed to provide support, defense, and aid. There was, for a Baluchi tribesman or tribeswoman living among his or her own, in his or her own territory, a sense of security. I do not want to exaggerate; each Baluch had his or her own personal and family needs and interests, and these did not always coincide with those of others. But each tribesman and tribeswoman had a right to claim support from the others, and the others felt both the moral obligation and the long-term practical benefit of maintaining lineage solidarity. Consequently, political action was group action, and social welfare measures were often collective as well. In contrast, Sardinian shepherds and their families, and other Sardinian highlanders, while situated in an exclusive comune which was their major social resource, had only thin social networks from which to call for aid. Nuclear families, following the rule of neo-local residence and living in separate houses, were somewhat encysted within themselves, and there was, aside from the common citizenship of the comune, immediate family ties, and the informal networks of friends, a degree of social fragmentation. As a result, political action tended to be carried out by individuals, sometimes with support from one or two others; in general, security rested upon the reputation of individuals and the implied threat of retailiation. So, certainly among the shepherds, there tended to be a feeling of insecurity, of standing alone against the world.

FEUDING AND VENDETTAS

In both tribal Baluchistan and highland Sardinia, the basic principle of social control, of insuring security against physical coercion, was retribution against an offense to person or property. The threat—and social peace usually depends upon a threat—is that no one can act against another man or his family or property without expecting in turn a violent response of equal or greater magnitude. In these societies, women and children were protected by the system of social control, and it was the men who were the designated agents of retribution; each man was expected to be a warrior and to fight if necessary. Physical prowess, combat skills, and bravery were important characteristics and highly respected. Honor and reputation depended upon the appropriate execution of retribution. To hold back from retribution in response to offense and injury, was to open oneself to further attacks, injuries, and losses.

The organization and process of retribution differed substantially in Baluchistan and Sardinia. In Baluchistan, through the institution of collective responsibility, the injured party and thus the party exacting retribution was always collective, a corporate lineage of greater or lesser size, depending upon the genealogical distance of the adversary. In Sardinia, the injured party was most commonly a single man and the family that depended upon him. In Baluchistan, conflict was overt, with the parties acting openly in the light of day. In Sardinia, attack was usually covert and furtive, with the perpetrator hidden and anonymous. In Baluchistan, a conflict and its details were public knowledge, while in Sardinia a conflict was deemed to be private knowledge, with all parties claiming ignorance. Finally, in Baluchistan, conflict generated mediation by structurally neutral parties, while in Sardinia the established principle was non-intervention by neutral parties. These differences in the operation of social control between Baluchistan and Sardinia were tied to differences in state presence.

ENCAPSULATION AND INCORPORATION

For both Baluchistan and Sardinia, the presence of the state, its institutions, and its agents was not the culmination of local political developments, reflecting local interests, intentions, and forces, but rather the result of intrusion of foreign power based externally and imposed through conquest. But between the two regions, there was a substantial difference in degree of state presence. Baluchistan had for centuries been on the far margins of Persian claims to suzerainty and beyond effective state control, when Reza Shah finally reconquered it in 1928–35, the major event in the modern history of Baluchistan. Baluchi tribes had for centuries been independent of state influence and operated as sovereign polities. They had even engaged with virtual impunity in predation against Persian subjects. After the conquest, the hand of the Persian state lay relatively lightly on Baluchistan, encapsulating the tribes but leaving their structures and institutions largely intact and interfering little in the local ways of making a living.

In contrast, for thousands of years Sardinia had been an imperial territory and colony, with one short break of independence and local rule. Imperial control of Sardinia went beyond encapsulation, with the controlling regimes effectively incorporating local peoples and resources into imperial institutions. Sometimes elements in Sardinian cities and lowland agricultural areas, usually organized into agricultural estates, *latifundi*, went beyond incorporation to assimilation, taking on the basic cultural characteristics of the conquerors.

The central highlands of Sardinia, Barbagia, was the least affected region, as the low density of people and resources made it less attractive to state officials, and the rugged landscape and rugged character of the people made it more trouble to control than it was worth. Mountains everywhere have served as a refuge from state intrusion, and mountain people tend to be resistant to external control, and intrepid in their defense of their independence (Boehm 1983). Highland Sardinians might have been moderately integrated into the state structure, but their level of assimilation into state politics has always been low. They have been more assimilated into other cultural realms associated with the state, such as the Roman Catholic Church. But the running of local affairs in highland Sardinia has tended to be constrained by but not assimilated to state practice.

The differences in social organization and political practice between Baluchistan and Sardinia were related to these differences in state influence. The light-handed state encapsulation of the Baluchi tribes left their nesting sets of corporate lineage groups intact, and they were able to continue to operate as defense and welfare organizations. In contrast, imperial incorporation of highland Sardinians did not permit the existence of organizations that did not correspond to imperial and state institutions. Corporate groups that were separate from state structures were deemed subversive and a threat to the state, which claimed the monopoly of physical coercion, and were suppressed. So without being able to form into ongoing support groups, Sardinians had to fall back on informal networks of friends.

In Baluchistan, conflict activated groups, sometimes large groups, and was overtly pursued, publicly known, and generated mediation. Even under Persian state encapsulation, there was no attempt to suppress these events, merely to limit them. In contrast, conflict in highland Sardinia was individually pursued, covert and furtive, and regarded by highlanders as a private matter, not to be interfered with by others. In contrast, the state regarded individual conflicts in highland Sardinia as its business, with the right to settle conflicts solely its own. Self-help by Sardinians was rigorously outlawed by state law. This is the reason that self-help by individual highland Sardinians in conflict was covert, secret, and studiously ignored by others. From a sociological and historical point of view, the local custom of silence can be understood as a defense against state authorities. Highland Sardinian forms of social control and justice deviated from state law, but the particular form of their deviation was shaped by a state presence strong enough to suppress local political organization but not effective enough to replace individual self-help.

LEVELING AND DEVELOPING

In highland Sardinia, rumors and character assassination, poison and bombs, and knives and shots were indicative of competition or retribution among local inhabitants or of resistance by locals against outsiders. But they could also reflect, intermingled with the other factors, envy, invidia, which was the individual sentiment tied to social leveling, or the defense of equality. Improvement, innovation, and entrepreneurship, processes that play an important part in economic change and expansion or development, were commonly seen among Sardinian highlanders as threats to community unity and the equality of community members. And so resistance to these kinds of changes were seen as defense of community values, community solidarity, and community equality. The result was, in highland Sardinian communities, a degree of resistance to change, to development, that frustrated and discouraged those people who wanted to try new things and improve themselves. This resistance to change acted as a spur to the emigration of innovators to more fertile, usually urban or mainland, locales. When those who wanted to change things left, and those who wanted to maintain things stayed, the result for highland communities was continuity rather than development and change. The danger was that the social, economic, and cultural gap that grew between the highland communities and urban centers would push young people, informed by school, mass media, and travel, to leave the highlands, thus consigning highland communities to eventual death or to be inhabited only during summer holidays by those who had moved elsewhere.

In Baluchistan the process was somewhat different. No one seemed to mind much if fellow tribesmen and tribeswomen tried new things and found innovative ways of creating wealth, such as marketing irrigation-grown watermelons, running a motorcycle taxi service, smuggling truckloads of tangerines, or guiding urbanites escaping the regime across the border. On the contrary, because the principle of tribal aid is "all for one, and one for all," if someone did well, so the local attitude seemed to be, everybody benefited. And this was indeed the scenario. If a Baluch was successful and did well, all relatives and lineage mates expected to benefit, to share, in the good fortune. So a tribesman with resources suffered continuous and intense demands from people to whom he had a moral obligation, and upon whom he might have to rely at some later time. In other words, among Baluchi tribesmen and tribeswomen, there was great pressure to share wealth, to distribute it among members of one's group. This cousin needed an animal for a wedding feast; that uncle needed a "loan" to go on the Haj to Mecca; that niece was ill and needed a contribution to travel to a hospital for an operation: all fair requests for worthy projects. The result was that building up and conserving capital, a necessary step in supporting a self-sustaining economic enterprise, was extraordinarily difficult due to the legitimate claims of *institutionalized reciprocity*. The economically ambitious Baluchi tribesman faced the unnerving choice of seeing his wealth dissipate among his fellows, or withdrawing from tribal obligations of reciprocity, with the associated moral stigma, loss of prestige, and potential political danger. In Baluchistan too, the path to development was full not only of economic obstacles, but ethical, social, and political ones as well.

CONCLUSION

In this brief excursion, I have been able to offer only a few comparisons of limited aspects of only two societies. But even this limited exercise can serve to indicate the power of comparison for eliciting broader perspectives and deeper insights. The juxtaposition of the Baluchi and Sardinian cases highlights differences and leads us to search for other aspects of the societies associated with these differences, which might help to explain why they have developed and what their consequences are.

If the ethnography of individual cases is primarily an exercise in description and interpretation, comparison of ethnographic cases is an exercise in explanation and generalization. In comparison we bring together two or more ethnographic cases in which certain events, such as migrations or feuds, are examined for their similarities and differences; then, we search for other events and contextual influences, such as seasonal changes or state control or informal social networks, which seem to underlie or follow from the events. We can then see whether similar precedents or consequents can be found for similar events, and whether differences in events and contextual influences give rise to, or follow from differences in events. For example, how did we understand differences in self-help vendettas and feuds, specifically the contrast between individual self-help in Sardinia and collective self-help in Baluchistan? We identified as a primary influence the suppression of local political groups in Sardinia by a state apparatus which had effectively incorporated highland communities into the state structure, in contrast with the more limited and more permissive encapsulation of Baluchi tribes by the Iranian state. As a result, in matters of coercion, Sardinians tended to act alone, while the Baluch continued to rely on their lineage-based, political action groups.

From such comparisons, we can draw more general formulations that serve as guides to further investigations. For example, following our discussion of self-help in Sardinia and Baluchistan, we would say that as state presence increases, coercive action by nonstate entities is suppressed. Furthermore, this contributes to a decline and disappearance of nonstate, regional and local defense groups and leadership roles. In other words, effective state presence leads to the destruction of other forms of political organization, such as tribes, lineages, chiefs, and city-states. What remains tends to be informal, private, and diffused, such as networks of "friends," and any coercive action is covert and kept secret.

Such substantive generalizations as this one about the consequences of strong state presence can and should be tested by the examination of other ethnographic cases, from Africa, Asia, and elsewhere, to see if these other cases conform to the generalization. If they do not, then whatever additional factor is complicating the picture can, in principle, be identified, and added as a qualification to the generalization. This kind of exploration and challenge by additional case material allows us to improve our general formulations, so that they apply more widely. At the same time, the testing and refinement of our substantive generalizations can provide us with confidence that our interpretation of our original case material was correct: We can have more confidence in our interpretations of individual cases if these have then been formulated more generally and been shown to hold up under challenge from other cases. So there is a kind of spiral in research, from the interpretation of individual cases, to comparisons of two or more cases, to substantive generalizations meant to apply to all similar cases, which, if validated by further comparison, reflect well on our initial interpretations. We thus spiral around from individual cases, to comparison, and back to individual cases, but with increased confidence in our understanding.

Chapter Five

An Anthropology
of Events

Events are delimited occurances that shape people's lives. On the one hand, many events are purposely instigated by people in particular positions acting to achieve their culturally and personally defined purposes. On the other hand, events also can arise from environmental forces or from other people's actions, sometimes taking on a life of their own and unexpectedly sweeping up people, even the initiators, and carrying them to unintended destinations. We have seen both aspects of events in our glimpses of life in a Middle Eastern desert and on a Mediterranean island.

In this chapter, we examine "an anthropology of events" as strategy and methodology in anthropological research. My intention is to show the usefulness in focusing on events and the advantages that this approach has over certain others, such as those which abstract and essentialize culture and position and those which limit anthropology to the study of words and discourses. But first, let us situate anthropology among those other students of events, journalists and historians.

JOURNALISM, HISTORY, AND ANTHROPOLOGY

Is an anthropology of events just a Johnny-come-lately, following in the well-worn footpaths of journalism and history, and does the anthropologist studying events become a kind of reporter of the trivial or historian of the exotic? Well, yes and no.

Journalistic attention to events is for the most part truncated by the necessities of immediate reporting, characterized by a simplification needed for the limited attention of the casual reader. It is restricted to the immediate events themselves, emphasizing the "current" in current events. Anthropologists prefer to investigate events for the insight that can be gained into people's lives and destinies, into the ways in which position and instituted meaning shape events and in turn are affected by them, through historical and cross-cultural comparison.

The modern study of history evolved from early chroniclers concerned with the simple recording of happenings that succeeded one another through time. Traditionally, historical studies have been different from anthropology in focusing on past rather than contemporary events and in depending upon written documentation as the primary evidence for understanding those events and their consequences. Historians share with anthropologists interest in the effects of events on people's lives. But traditionally historians were more interested in the flow of events through time than the arrangements of position and the frameworks of meaning, which provided at least the context and sometimes the impetus of events and which were themselves affected by the events. Increasingly throughout the twentieth century, however, historians have drawn upon anthropological and social scientific perspectives, adopting a fuller treatment of position and meaning, and thus initiating from its side a convergence between historical and anthropological studies.

Anthropology, for its part, has found its earlier, synchronic, "snap-shot" pictures of societies and cultures to be static and unrealistic and has moved to a more historical approach, placing in time, in dated, temporal sequence, the people and events, arrangements of position and frameworks of meaning it studies, and treating culture and positional frameworks as part of ongoing processes rather than as timeless, eternal verities. The anthropology of events is a manifestation of this convergence between anthropological and historical orientations and marries the strengths of both. Some anthropologists, such as Moore (1987: 730 and passim; 1994), have argued that ethnographic research should be cast as an exploration of "current history."

PROBLEMS OF ABSTRACTION AND ESSENTIALISM

We anthropologists rely on abstraction to move beyond the confusing welter of daily life and its infinite variety of particulars. In order to grasp the main components of how people structure their lives and communicate them clearly, we have intellectually stepped back from individuals and their lives and abstracted structures of positions and systems of cultural concepts and values. We are most comfortable when we can sum up people and their diverse situations by talking about "culture patterns," "deep structures," "class systems," and "gender hierarchies." As well, we often seem to treat one main cultural feature or social arrangement as the "essence" of a people's lives. These abstract formulations have sometimes been insightful and brilliant, and they undoubtedly have advanced our understanding.

But there are three serious interrelated problems with this abstract way of thinking about people and their lives. One is that we often end up reifying "culture" and "position" by treating these cognitive abstractions of ours as if they were forces that made people do one thing or another. Ishvar and Omprakash were not driven from their village by "the caste system," but by their desire to better themselves and by the resentment and anger of certain upper caste members who saw the pair's aspirations as an offense and a threat. Reification thus misrepresents reality by distracting us from the specific motives and actions, and circumstances and conditions, that activate people and those around them.

A second problem is that these general formulations usually posit homogeneous, unitary, and logically consistent cultures and position structures, whereas the reality that people live with—whether in desert bands, mountain tribes, agrarian plains, or crowded cities—is always to a significant degree variable, fragmented, and inconsistent (Moore 1987:729–30). For example, in spite of Ishvar and Omprakash's membership in the Chamaar tanners' and leather workers' caste, they were in fact trained and working as tailors. This anomaly shows that the elegant consistency of conception seldom corresponds to the inconsistencies and contradictions of reality. For this reason, abstract formulations, such as "the caste system," usually go beyond simplifying to *over*simplifying, leaving us without a good guide to the complex and often contradictory reality of people's lives.

Similarly, we have seen in the tribal deserts that local culture is not so much a highly integrated complex of elements forming a seamless, unitary whole, as it is a limited set of diverse and alternative ways of thinking, assessing, relating to space, responding to the environment, organizing people, making a living, establishing security, dealing with threats, and thus dealing with the flow of events. These alternative cultural modes, these multiplicities, are not indicative of cultural malintegration or disintegration, but rather of instituted flexibility making possible a dynamic response to the flow of events in a changing, shifting environment.

Third, abstract conceptions of culture and of position tend to be static, describing set features and relationships in permanent patterns. But real people live in time, and through time things sometimes change, including cultural conceptions and values and positions in sets of relationships. The Chamaar untouchable caste had been given the right to vote in the constitution of India and their names were on voters' lists.

Their vote was in principle equal to that of members of the upper, "clean" castes. This was a great break with the way the system had operated in the past. True, in practice, the votes of members of untouchable castes were often stolen. Indeed, attempts by members of those castes to exercise their rights as citizens of a constitutional state were often thwarted, sometimes by brutal violence, especially in rural communities, as Mistry graphically describes in his account of the 1970s in India. But India in 1970 was a very different place from India in 1870, and "the caste system" of 1970 operated in a different social, cultural, and political context from "the caste system" of 1870. "Caste" today is not what it once was (Kolenda [1978] 1985), and the destiny of each person as a caste member is different from what it was before. An examination of the events of 1970s India allows Mistry to explore not only what the caste system was at that time, but also the pressures of the constitutional polity on the caste system; we can see the caste system not only in its being, but also in its becoming.

The anthropology of events, or, perhaps more accurately, doing anthropology through the study of events, is a distinguished tradition in modern anthropology. It developed strongly in the 1960s to provide insight into social dynamics and cultural change, and was conceived as a focus on social and cultural *processes*, sequences of events such as decision making, conflict resolution, and transactions and exchanges between individuals and groups. From this point of view, especially in the theoretically powerful work of Fredrik Barth (1967), meaning and position, rather than being fixed and based upon norms, often arose from processes, rather than the other way around. Furthermore, among the many existing rules or norms in any culture, more than one is conceivably applicable in any particular situation, and each of them is vague enough to be open to various interpretations. This gives individuals and groups in any society considerable leeway for pursuing their own interests or agendas, which means that the significance of particular norms can be best studied "situationally," within the contexts in which they are invoked by people (Van Velsen 1967). For this reason, there has been a shift of emphasis among mainstream anthropologists from formulating abstractions of structure and culture to the examination of events (Moore 1987:729 and passim, 1994; Vayda 1994; Barth 1994).

Barth ([1961] 1986) shows, for example, in his brilliant account of the *Nomads of South Persia*, that tribes and tribal confederations are not "natural" entities arising from kinship ties, although tribal societies often like to use a kinship idiom, but rather the result of conscious strategies, negotiated deals, and contractual agreements, often in response to particular events or series of events. The Khamseh tribal confederation that Barth describes was instigated by urban merchants who wanted to secure their caravans against the raiding and extortion of another tribal confederation. The tribal chiefs joining in the confederation were unified by a generous glue of expensive gifts, including armaments, from the merchants. Another example is the way in which the political loyalty and consent of tribesmen and tribeswomen to the "omnipotent" rule of their chief was generated and maintained by the ongoing processes of exchange of views and testing of public opinion by the chief, so that he would not violate the expectations and wishes of his followers (Salzman Forthcoming A).

TALK AND ACTION

Some recent anthropological thought (e.g., Clifford and Marcus 1986; Marcus 1994) has challenged the appropriateness, validity, and even morality of an "anthropology of events"—of ethnographic description, interpretation, and explanation. Some argue that it should be replaced by an anthropology of "voice," in which people from other cultures speak directly for themselves and research reports consist mainly of interview transcripts, sometimes from only one informant (e.g., Crapanzano 1980; Lavie 1990). The rationale underlying this critique of traditional ethnographic research, including the stream that I have called the anthropology of events, combines several arguments. One is the so-called "problem of representation," which questions the right of an ethnographer, especially a foreign ethnographer, to speak of the lives of others. Accounts by foreign researchers are, so the argument goes, a kind of illegitimate appropriation of the soul of the cultural "other," a kind of symbolic rape.

A second argument, which supports the first argument, is that ethnographic researchers are not objective observers of objects because researchers are seeing other cultures through their own subjectivities and because other people cannot be understood as objects, but only as subjects, the subjects of their own lives. Thus an honest account, so the argument goes, can only present the subjectivity of the native subject rather than impose the subjectivity of the foreign researchers. This argument depends upon extreme "epistemological relativism," which asserts that there is no basis for judging the truth of any viewpoint or opinion, so all accounts have to be considered equally valid.

A third argument, which supports the others, is that foreign researchers are usually from powerful countries, countries with histories of and current involvement in imperialism and colonialism, and that the people and peoples studied are usually members of the oppressed, "subaltern" classes of the exploited Third and Fourth Worlds. Thus, as a matter of political morality, researchers should not be distanced, uninvolved observers but should be active, engaged supporters of the subaltern classes and oppressed peoples and countries. From this perspective, the important question is not what can one discover, but whose cause can one advocate.

It is for these reasons that some philosophers, literary critics, and anthropologists argue that we must focus exclusively on the "word," on what people, informants, say about themselves. This—so the argument goes—allows the anthropologist to treat people as "subjects" rather than as "objects" of research, to make it possible for our subjects to have their own voices, and thus to be free of domination by the researcher and what she or he represents. This strategy of focusing on the "word" and giving "voice" allows the researcher to jettison epistemological claims of naturalistic, scientific objectivity, which are deemed unjustifiable, and at the same time to relinquish colonialist, imperialist suppression and oppression of the informant by the author and her or his research penetration and authorial authority.

It appears to me that this focus on the "word" arose from the interpretive, symbolic anthropology of Geertz (1973), which emphasized culture as a system of meaning and defined research as the interpretation of meaning. It was taken to its logical conclusion of "voice" by extreme epistemological relativism and its associated anti-imperialist and pro-subaltern commitments, which directed the researcher to attend exclusively to the pronouncements of selected informants, generating as research findings interview protocol texts.

With this approach and its focus on what people say about themselves, preferred research topics must shift away from what happens in the world, about which individual informants are not necessarily informed or reliable commentators, to subjects such as what and how people think about themselves, their self-concept, identity, and body image and about their personal experience, the abuse they have received, and their suffering (e.g., Marcus 1994). While these are all legitimate and important topics, exclusive attention to them has narrowed considerably the range and reliability of anthropological research. Considering its serious undermining of the broad anthropological vision, we might wonder whether the shift to extreme subjectivism is going farther than necessary. To many mainstream anthropologists (e.g., Gellner 1992; Barth 1994), including myself, this approach seems extreme and counterproductive.

The greatest weakness of the exclusive emphasis on "meaning" and "voice" is that, while it gives us a good idea of what people will say to anthropologists, what pronouncements it pleases them to make, which self-image they wish to present to us, we have little way of knowing what people will actually do, how they will act, in their encounters in the real world. Interviews do not give us a very good idea what our informants say to other people, such as their relatives, neighbors, and fellow workers, in the course of their real lives. And can we even be sure that what they say to us is what they truly believe? While it is somewhat misleading to say that "actions speak louder than words," for speaking is a kind of action, and speaking itself often has a great impact, nonetheless, an anthropology that attends only to words and never to actions surely is more one-sided than it need be. It is also much less capable than a more balanced approach of grasping and understanding the complex reality of people's lives. Some researchers, including those who earlier took rather extreme positions, have begun to appreciate this (e.g., Marcus 1995).

Anthropologists concerned with social process and change have sought ways to investigate human beings in action. One research procedure to advance the study of process was developed and deployed effectively by the Manchester University school of anthropology. This approach, sometimes called "the extended case method" or "situational analysis" (Gluckman 1961; Van Velsen 1967), focuses on events, such as decision making, alliances, and conflicts, and includes in the study of tribal societies such instances as witchcraft accusations, marriage alliances, chiefly legislation, succession to a throne, and blood feuds. The researcher focuses on whatever event is taking place, considering it situationally by placing it in the context of previous events, following along the various stages of the event as it unfolds. The researcher considers the consequences of the event on the lives of the people involved and the impact of the event on the subsequent arrangements of position and on the understood and accepted cultural meanings. Especially informative for indicating possible future developments are "diagnostic events" which reveal "ongoing contests and conflicts and competitions and the efforts to prevent, suppress, or repress these" and thus indicate basic pressures in society (Moore 1987:730).

By observing people "in action," extended case study analysis facilitates learning about the often conflicting points of view and understandings of the various people involved in the event examined and how these are drawn from and feed back into rules, norms, and cultural meanings. In extended case study analysis we go far beyond the comments of single informants in artificial interview contexts, for it is impossible to know what "voice," freed in the interview situation from the processes of real life, represents beyond contextless words. Furthermore, in the study of events, the anthropologist, taking into account the various points of view held by the participating actors and indigenous observers, must himself or herself take responsibility for describing the complex reality (Barth 1994). This responsibility for presenting a general ethnographic picture based upon information from many informants and upon many types of observation and documentation cannot be evaded by the serious anthropologist. Indeed, an alternative, post-modern strategy of offering only interview protocols, on the grounds that they are a record of an authentic indigenous "voice," is no more than an epistemologically rationalized dereliction of responsibility.

"EVENTS" IN ANTHROPOLOGY

The anthropology of events is not a new theory or new approach; it is not a revolution in perspective nor a "paradigm shift." After all, "events have long been a basic part of ethnographic data" (Moore 1987:729). Rather, an anthropology of events is the expression of an approach which we have found to be sound and fruitful, insightful and true to life in the study of human lives.

Many ethnographic accounts illustrating this event-oriented approach are now considered "classics," such as Evans-Pritchard's (1949) ethnography of the response of the Bedouin and the Sanusi sufi order to the Italian invasion of Libya; Gluckman's (1955) presentation of the Barotse people through their court cases; Mitchell's (1956a) account of witchcraft accusations and divinations and the split of a village into two villages, as well as his (1956b) exploration of life among urban Africans through the examination of a "tribal" dance; Turner's (1957) description of a set of interrelated events he calls "social dramas" and how they feed into the developmental cycles of African villages; and Cohen's (1969) report on an urban ethnic community's religious conversion as a way of maintaining group unity in newly independent Nigeria. The value of this focus on events is equally illustrated by contemporary ethnographies, such as McCabe's (1994) report on the effects of repeated droughts on the pastoral tribes of East Africa; Dubisch's (1995) entry into Greek life through an exploration of the pilgrimage to an island shrine; Peters' (1994) exploration of "politics, policy, and culture in Botswana," and especially access to grazing land, through following the competition during 1979–80 among syndicates of cattle owners who controlled boreholes; Meneley's (1996) examination of class and gender in a Middle Eastern town through recounting the unending sequence of segregated parties; Galaty's (1994) presentation of the imposition of "group ranches" and related struggles over land among the Maasai in East Africa; and Chatty's (1996) account of the arrival of oil exploration in the desert of Oman and its impact on the regional nomadic tribe. The anthropology of events has a distinguished history, and has proven to be a fruitful entrée into an understanding of people's lives.

The reason for the success of these anthropological accounts is that they are well grounded in a broad range of information drawn from many different sources. By focusing their long-term, ethnographic field research on events, these anthropological researchers have been led

> to observe people's actions in their natural settings, where people are interacting with each other about matters important to their lives;

> to listen to what people say to each other in the course of their real lives;

> to discuss directly with individuals their relationships with the other people involved, their reasons for acting as they did, and their understanding of the significance of this or that happening;

> to collect from different persons their similar or different versions of the happenings;

> to ask about other similar or different incidents, or previous or contemporaneous incidents related in the minds of participants and local observers to the events in question;

> to examine relevant documentation, such as legal texts, records of court cases, documents of ownership or contracts of agreement, and birth, marriage, and death records;

> and to relate the event under examination to other observed events, whether contemporaneous, previous, or subsequent, that involve some of the same people, that appear related to the events under question, or that independently influence people's lives and shape position and meaning in ways parallel to or otherwise than the events under question.

When compared to other more restricted approaches, this approach to information collection from different sources provides a richer and sounder body of information to work with in understanding people's lives. No single source of information, such as formal interviews with individuals (favored by postmodern, "dialogical" anthropologists), or surveys or questionnaires (favored by sociologists), can begin to provide a soundly based understanding of people's lives. Other, more "philosophical" or "critical" approaches, such as the deconstruction favored by so-called "cultural studies," or the reflections of "ethics" specialists often provide little basis for understanding and tend to emphasize moralizing and political propaganda rather than learning.

The anthropology of events is thus the study of "position" and "culture" in action, through which the real substance of these can be understood, as well as the study of the shaping of lives, position and culture, by the sweep of events. An emphasis on events, as they arise from and shape cultural meaning and relational position, focuses on people's actions and activities as they pursue their goals, deal with other people, and cope with circumstances and conditions as they arise and shift through time. Position in action becomes power and constraint, just as meaning in action becomes intention and orientation. Furthermore, events take place amidst the interplay among many different influences and forces, and the part played by position, for example in the caste system, interacts with the part played by culture, as in the understanding of ritual purity and pollution, which interacts with the understanding of citizens' rights in a constitutional democracy. Our abstractions of the caste system and constitutional rights show us the internal logic of each, but to see how they work out in everyday practice and how they affect people's lives and destinies, we must see how they interact in actual events and how they play out over the course of events through time.

In sum, the study of events is particularly useful in the attempt to understand human beings and their lives. Events arise from what people do and are what happens to them. By examining particular events we are able to focus on the specific ways in which people's real lives are expressed, advanced, enhanced, distorted, disrupted, and terminated. This is why I argue that the study of events is the anthropology of real life.

References

Abella, Irving, and Harold Troper. 1982. *None Is Too Many: Canada and the Jews of Europe 1933–1948*. Toronto: Lester and Orpen Dennys.

Arfa, General Hassan. 1964. *Under Five Shahs*. London: John Murray.

Assmuth, Laura. 1997. *Women's Work, Women's Worth: Changing Lifecourses in Highland Sardinia*. Transactions No. 39. Helsinki: Finnish Anthropological Society.

Bailey, F. G. 1969. *Stratagems and Spoils: A Social Anthropology of Politics*. Oxford: Basil Blackwell.

Barfield, Thomas J. 1993. *The Nomadic Alternative*. Englewood Cliffs, NJ: Prentice Hall.

Barth, Fredrik. 1967. *Models of Social Organization*. Occasional Paper No. 23. London: Royal Anthropological Institute.

_____. [1961] 1986. *Nomads of South Persia*. Prospect Heights, IL: Waveland Press.

_____. 1994. A Personal View of Present Tasks and Priorities in Cultural and Social Anthropology. In *Assessing Cultural Anthropology*, edited by R. Borofsky. New York: McGraw-Hill.

Bates, Daniel. 1973. *Nomads and Farmers: A Study of the Yörük of Southeastern Turkey*. Anthropological Papers No. 52, Museum of Anthropology, University of Michigan, Ann Arbor.

Beck, Lois. 1991. *Nomad: a Year in the Life of a Qashqa'i Tribesman in Iran*. Berkeley: University of California Press.

_____. Forthcoming. *Nomads Move On*.

Bellow, Saul. [1987] 1997. *More Die of Heartbreak*. New York: Dell.

Boehm, Christopher. 1983. The Political Ecology of Refuge Area Warriors, *Nomadic Peoples*, no. 12:4–13.

Boissevain, Jeremy. 1974. *Friends of Friends: Networks, Manipulators and Coalitions*. Oxford: Basil Blackwell.

Burghart, R. 1978. Hierarchical Models of the Hindu Social System, *Man* (N.S.) 13:519–36.

Caltagirone, Benedetto. 1989. *Animali Perduti: Abigeato e Scambio Sociale in Barbagia*. Cagliari: Celt Editrice.

Camarda, Ignazio. 1992. Un Parco Naturale per il Gennargentu. In *Il Parco del Gennargentu: Un'Occasione da Non Perdere*. Cagliari: TEMA.

Cao, Mario Franco. 1995. Liberate Vinci e Sircana, *L'Unione Sarda*, 12 May, p. 12.

Chatty, Dawn. 1986. *From Camel to Truck: The Bedouin in the Modern World*. New York: Vantage.

_____. 1996. *Mobile Pastoralists: Development Planning and Social Change in Oman*. New York: Columbia University Press.

Clifford, James, and George E. Marcus, eds. 1986. *Writing Culture: The Poetics and Politics of Ethnography*. Berkeley: University of California Press.

Cocco, Flavio. 1986. *Dati Relativi alla Storia dei Paesi della Diocesi d'Ogliastra, Vol. III: Talana, Tertenia, Tortolì, Triei, Ulassai, Urzulei, Ussassa, Villagrande Strisaili, Villaputzu*. Caligari: Tipografia TEA.

Cohen, Abner. 1969. *Custom and Politics in Urban Africa*. Berkeley: University of California Press.

Corriere della Sera. Daily newspaper. Published in Italy.

Crapanzano, Vincent. 1980. *Tuhami: Portrait of a Moroccan*. Chicago: University of Chicago Press.

De Gioannis, Paola, and Giuseppe Serri, eds. 1991. *La Sardegna: Cultura e Società*. Firenze: La Nuova Italia.

Dubisch, Jill. 1995. *In a Different Place: Pilgrimage, Gender, and Politics at a Greek Island Shrine*. Princeton: Princeton University Press.

Dyer, Brigadier-General R. E. H. 1921. *The Raiders of the Sarhad: Being an Account of a Campaign of Arms and Bluff Against the Brigands of the Persian-Baluchi Border During the Great War*. London: Witherby.

Edelsward, Lisa Marlene. 1988. Communities of Conflict and Cooperation. Working Paper of the Mediterranean Anthropological Research Equipe, Department of Anthropology, McGill University, Montreal.

_____. 1995. *Highland Visions: Recreating Rural Sardinia*. Ph.D. dissertation. Montreal: McGill University.

Eggan, Fred. 1954. Social Anthropology and the Method of Controlled Comparison, *American Anthropologist* 56(5): 743–63.

Evans-Pritchard, E. E. 1940. *The Nuer*. Oxford: Clarendon Press.

_____. 1949. *The Sanusi of Cyrenaica*. Oxford: Clarendon Press.

Fabietti, Ugo, and P.C. Salzman, eds. 1996. *The Anthropology of Tribal and Peasant Pastoral Societies*. Pavia, Italy: Collegio Ghislieri; Como, Italy: Ibis.

Fiori, Giuseppe. 1978. *Baroni in Laguna: La Società del Malessere*. Bari, Laterza. Extract reprinted in *La Sardegna: Cultura e Società*, edited by Paola De Gioannis and Giuseppe Serri. Firenze: La Nuova Italia, 1991.

Floris, Vincenzo. 1995. Il Volto Buono del Nuorese, *L'Unione Sarda*, 16 May, p. 2.

Foster, George M. 1965. Peasant Society and the Image of Limited Good, *American Anthropologist* 67:293–315.

Galaty, John G. 1994. Rangeland Tenure and Pastoralism in Africa. In *African Pastoralist Systems*, edited by Elliot Fratkin, K. A. Galvin, and E. A. Roth. Boulder: Lynne Rienner.

Galaty, John G., and Douglas L. Johnson, eds. 1990. *The World of Pastoralism: Herding Systems in Comparative Perspective*. New York: Guilford Press.

Geertz, Clifford. 1973. *The Interpretation of Cultures*. New York: Basic Books.

Gellner, Ernest. 1988. *Plough, Sword and Book: The Structure of Human History*. Chicago: University of Chicago Press.

_____. 1992. *Postmodernism, Reason and Religion*. London: Routledge.

Gluckman, Max. 1955. *The Judicial Process among the Barotse of Northern Rhodesia*. Manchester: Manchester University Press.

_____. 1961. Ethnographic Data in British Social Anthropology, *Sociological Review* 9:5–17.

Goldhagen, Daniel Jonah. 1996. *Hitler's Willing Executioners*. New York: Knopf.

Heatherington, Tracey. 1993. *Environmental Politics in a Highland Sardinian Community*. Master's thesis, McGill University.

Irons, William. 1975. *The Yomut Turkmen*. Anthropological Papers No. 58, Museum of Anthropology, University of Michigan, Ann Arbor.

ISTAT (Istituto Nazionale di Statistica [of Italy]). 1986. *Sommario di Statistiche Storiche 1926–1985*. Roma: ISTAT.

_____. 1991. *Le Regioni in Cifre*. Roma: ISTAT.

Keesing, Roger. 1994. Theories of Culture Revisited. In *Assessing Cultural Anthropology*, edited by R. Borofsky. New York: McGraw-Hill.

Kolenda, Pauline. [1978] 1985. *Caste in Contemporary India: Beyond Organic Solidarity*. Prospect Heights, IL: Waveland Press.

Lavie, Smadar. 1990. *The Poetics of Military Occupation: Mzeina Allegories of Bedouin Identity under Israeli and Egyptian Rule*. Berkeley: University of California Press.

Liori, Antonangelo. 1991. *Manuale di Sopravvivenza in Barbagia*. Cagliari: Edizioni della Torre.

_____. 1995. Complicità Invidia e Vergogna, *L'Unione Sarda*, 15 May, p. 1.

Malthus, Thomas. [1798] 1959. *Population: The First Essay*. Ann Arbor: University of Michigan Press. (*Essay on the Principle of Population* was originally published in 1798.)

Marcus, George E. 1994. After the Critique of Ethnography: Faith, Hope, and Charity, but the Greatest of These Is Charity. In *Assessing Cultural Anthropology*, edited by R. Borofsky. New York: McGraw-Hill.

_____. 1995. Ethnography in/of the World System: The Emergence of Multi-sited Ethnography, *Annual Review of Anthropology* 24:95–117.

McCabe, J. Terrence. 1994. Mobility and Land Use among African Pastoralists. In *African Pastoralist Systems*, edited by Elliot Fratkin, K. A. Galvin, and E. A. Roth. Boulder: Lynne Rienner.

Meneley, Anne. 1996. *Tournaments of Power: Sociability and Hierarchy in a Yemeni Town*. Toronto: University of Toronto Press.

Mistry, Rohinton. 1995. *A Fine Balance*. Toronto: McClelland and Stewart.

Mitchell, J. Clyde. 1956a. *The Yao Village: a Study in the Social Structure of a Nyasaland Tribe*. Manchester: Manchester University Press.

_____. 1956b. *The Kalela Dance*. Rhodes-Livingstone Papers, No. 27. Manchester: Manchester University Press.

Moore, Sally Falk. 1987. Explaining the Present: Theoretical Dilemmas in Processual Ethnography, *American Ethnologist* 14(4): 727–36.

_____. 1994. The Ethnography of the Present and the Analysis of Process. In *Assessing Cultural Anthropology*, edited by R. Borofsky. New York: McGraw-Hill.

Murgia, Costantino. 1992. Il Parco Nazionale del Gennargentu: Aspetti Giuridici. In *Il Parco del Gennargentu: Un'Occasione da Non Perdere*. Cagliari: TEMA.

Nadel, S. F. 1952. Witchcraft in Four African Societies: An Essay in Comparison, *American Anthropologist* 54(1): 18–29.

Nader, Laura. 1994. Comparative Consciousness. In *Assessing Cultural Anthropology*, edited by R. Borofsky. New York: McGraw-Hill.

Natali, Anna. 1992. Tutela e Sviluppo. In *Il Parco del Gennargentu: Un'Occasione da non Perdere*, Cagliari: TEMA.

Nieddu, Gianni, Antonio Uda, and Gino Mereu. 1995. Assuefazione ai Sequestri, *L'Unione Sarda*, 19 May, p. 3.

Nuova Sardegna, La. Daily newspaper. Published in Sasseri, Sardinia.

Ortner, Sherry. 1973. On Key Symbols, *American Anthropologist* 75(5): 1338–46.

Panorama. National weekly news magazine. Published in Milan.

Peters, Pauline E. 1994. *Dividing the Commons: Politics, Policy, and Culture in Botswana*. Charlottesville: University Press of Virginia.

Pigliaru, Antonio. 1975. *Il Banditismo in Sardegna: La Vendetta Barbaricina come Ordinamento Giuridico*. Milano: Giuffrè Editore.

Pititu, Gianni. 1995. Ma È Sbagliato Reagire a Testa Bassa, *L'Unione Sarda*, 16 May, p. 3.

Sahlins, Marshall. 1961. The Segmentary Lineage: An Organization of Predatory Expansion. *American Anthropologist* 63:322–43.

Salzman, Philip Carl. 1978a. Does Complementary Opposition Exist? *American Anthropologist* 80:53–70.

_____. 1978b. Ideology and Change in Tribal Society, *Man* (N.S.)13, 618–37.

_____. 1981. Culture as Enhabilmentis. In *The Structure of Folk Models*, edited by L. Holy and M. Stuchlik. A.S.A. Monograph 20, London, Academic Press, pp. 233–56.

_____. 1992. *Kin and Contract in Baluchi Herding Camps*. Baluchistan Monogaph Series II. Naples: Istituto Universitario Orientale, and Istituto Italiano per il Medio ed Estremo Oriente.

_____. 1996a. Peasant Pastoralists. In *The Anthropology of Tribal and Peasant Pastoral Societies*, edited by Ugo Fabietti and P. C. Salzman. Pavia: Collegio Ghislieri; Como: Ibis.

_____. 1996b. The Electronic Trojan Horse: Television in the Globalization of Paramodern Cultures. In *The Cultural Dimensions of Global Change: An Anthropological Approach*, edited by Lourdes Arizpe. Paris: UNESCO.

_____. Forthcoming A. Hierarchical Image and Reality: The Construction of a Tribal Chiefship, *Comparative Studies in Society and History*.

_____. Forthcoming B. *Black Tents of Baluchistan*. Washington, DC: Smithsonian Institution Press.

Scuola di Pubblica Amministrazione e Governo Locale di Nuoro and Assessorato all'Ambiente della Provincia di Nuoro. 1992. *Un parco del Gennargentu: Un'Occasione da Non Perdere*. Cagliari: TEMA.

Solinas, Pier Giorgio. 1989. *Pastori Sardi in Provincia di Siena*, Volumes I, II, & III. Siena, Italy: Laboratorio Etno-Antropologico, Università degli Studi di Siena.

Solinas, Pier Giorgio, Sandra Becucci, and Simonetta Grilli. 1996. Migrant Shepherds: From Sardinia to Tuscany. In *The Anthropology of Tribal and Peasant Pastoral Societies*, edited by Ugo Fabietti and P. C. Salzman. Pavia: Collegio Ghislieri; Como: Ibis.

Turner, Victor. 1957. *Schism and Continuity in an African Society*. Manchester: Manchester University Press.

Unione Sarda, L'. Daily newspaper. Published in Cagliari, Sardinia.

Van Velsen, J. 1967. The Extended-Case Method and Situational Analysis. In *The Craft of Social Anthropology*, edited by A. L. Epstein. London: Tavistock Publications.

Vayda, Andrew P. 1994. Actions, Variations, and Change: The Emerging Anti-Essentialist View in Anthropology. In *Assessing Cultural Anthropology*, edited by R. Borofsky. New York: McGraw-Hill.

Wolf, Eric. 1994. Facing Power. In *Assessing Cultural Anthropology*, edited by Robert Borofsky. New York: McGraw-Hill.

Zene, Cosimo. 1996. "Handloom Weavers of Nule, Sardinia: Between Art Production and Economic Enterprise." Paper presented at the Conference of the European Association of Social Anthropologists, Barcelona.

Index

•